Lincoln Comes to Gettysburg

THE CREATION OF THE SOLDIERS' NATIONAL CEMETERY AND LINCOLN'S GETTYSBURG ADDRESS

Bradley M. Gottfried and
Linda I. Gottfried

EMERGING CIVIL WAR SERIES

Chris Mackowski, series editor
Chris Kolakowski, chief historian

The Emerging Civil War Series

offers compelling, easy-to-read overviews of some of the Civil War's most important battles and stories.

Recipient of the Army Historical Foundation's Lieutenant General Richard G. Trefry Award for contributions to the literature on the history of the U.S. Army

Also part of the Emerging Civil War Series:

Don't Give an Inch: The Second Day at Gettysburg, July 2, 1863—from Little Round Top to Cemetery Ridge by Chris Mackowski, Kristopher D. White, and Daniel T. Davis

Fight Like the Devil: The First Day at Gettysburg, July 1, 1863 by Chris Mackowski, Kristopher D. White, and Daniel T. Davis

Hellmira: The Union's Most Infamous Civil War Prison Camp, Elmira, N.Y. by Derek Maxfield

Out Flew the Sabres: The Battle of Brandy Station, June 9, 1863 by Eric J. Wittenberg and Daniel T. Davis

The Last Road North: A Guide to the Gettysburg Campaign, 1863 by Robert Orrison and Dan Welch

Also by Bradley M. Gottfried and Linda I. Gottfried:

Hell Comes to Southern Maryland: The History of the Point Lookout Prisoner of War Camp

Also by Bradley M. Gottfried:

Kearny's Own: The History of the First New Jersey Brigade
Maps of First Bull Run
Maps of Antietam
Maps of the Fredericksburg
Maps of Gettysburg
Maps of the Cavalry at Gettysburg
Maps of Bristoe Station/Mine Run
Maps of the Wilderness Campaign
Roads to Gettysburg
Stopping Pickett: The History of the Philadelphia Brigade
The Artillery of Gettysburg
The Battle of Gettysburg: A Guided Tour
The Brigades of Gettysburg

For a complete list of titles in the Emerging Civil War Series, visit www.emergingcivilwar.com.

Lincoln Comes to Gettysburg

THE CREATION OF THE SOLDIERS' NATIONAL CEMETERY AND LINCOLN'S GETTYSBURG ADDRESS

Bradley M. Gottfried and
Linda I. Gottfried

EMERGING CIVIL WAR SERIES

SB

Savas Beatie
California

First edition, first printing

ISBN-13 (paperback): 978-1-61121-559-5
ISBN-13 (ebook): 978-1-61121-560-1

Library of Congress Cataloging-in-Publication Data

Names: Gottfried, Bradley M., author. | Gottfried, Linda I., author.
Title: Lincoln comes to Gettysburg : the creation of the Soldiers' National
    Cemetery and Lincoln's Gettysburg Address / by Bradley M. Gottfried and
    Linda I. Gottfried.
Other titles: Creation of the Soldiers' National Cemetery and Lincoln's
    Gettysburg Address
Description: El Dorado Hills, CA : Savas Beatie, [2020] | Includes
    bibliographical references. | Summary: "After almost 8,000 dead dotted
    the fields of Gettysburg, several men hatched the idea of a new cemetery
    to bury and honor the Union soldiers just south of town. Their task was
    difficult to say the least. This book recounts the events surrounding
    the creation of the Soldiers' National Cemetery, its dedication, and
    concentrates on Lincoln's visit to Gettysburg on November 18-19, 1863"--
    Provided by publisher.
Identifiers: LCCN 2020037820 | ISBN 9781611215595 (paperback) | ISBN
    9781611215601 (ebook)
Subjects: LCSH: Soldiers' National Cemetery (Gettysburg, Pa.)--History. |
    Soldiers' bodies, Disposition
    of--Pennsylvania--Gettysburg--History--19th century. | United
    States--History--Civil War,
    1861-1865--Casualties--Pennsylvania--Gettysburg. | Gettysburg, Battle
    of, Gettysburg, Pa., 1863. | Lincoln, Abraham, 1809-1865. Gettysburg
    address.
Classification: LCC E475.55 .G68 2020 | DDC 973.7/349--dc23
LC record available at https://lccn.loc.gov/2020037820

Published by
Savas Beatie LLC
989 Governor Drive, Suite 102
El Dorado Hills, California 95762
Phone: 916-941-6896
Email: sales@savasbeatie.com
Web: www.savasbeatie.com

Savas Beatie titles are available at special discounts for bulk purchases in the United States by corporations, institutions, and other organizations. For more details, please contact Special Sales, P.O. Box 4527, El Dorado Hills, CA 95762, or you may e-mail us at sales@savasbeatie.com, or visit our website at www.savasbeatie.com for additional information.

To the men who fought and died at Gettysburg

The world will little note, nor long remember what we say here, but it can never forget what they did here. It is for us the living, rather, to be dedicated here to the unfinished work which they who fought here have thus far so nobly advanced.
Abraham Lincoln, November 19, 1863

And

To our brothers who died far too soon
Dennis Gottfried
Michael Voglis

Table of Contents

List of Maps

Maps by Bradley M. Gottfried

Footnotes for this volume are available at
https://emergingcivilwar.com/publications/the-emerging-civil-war-series/footnotes/

For the Emerging Civil War Series

Theodore P. Savas, *publisher*
Chris Mackowski, *series editor*
Christopher Kolakowski, *chief historian*
Sarah Keeney, *editorial consultant*
Kristopher D. White, *co-founding editor*

Publication supervision by Chris Mackowski
Design and layout by Savannah Rose

Acknowledgments

More books have been written about Abraham Lincoln than any other United States president. His every action has been scrutinized and memorialized. Lincoln's visit to Gettysburg ranks high among his many legacies. Since Brad has written several books on Gettysburg and has a strong interest in the subject, we thought it a good idea to tell the story of the interface between the battle, the death and burial of so many young men, the Soldiers Cemetery creation, and Lincoln's immortal visit. Many books have been written about Lincoln's visit, but they tend to be ponderous and academic. Many fewer have tackled the interface of the topics addressed above. Thanks to ACHS staff members Tim Smith

An aluminum tablet features the act of Congress that established national cemeteries. (cm)

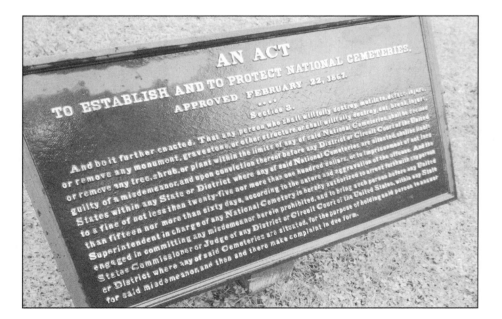

and Maria Lynn for their assistance, as well.

This book could not have been written without the support of a number of individuals. John Heiser of Gettysburg National Military Park was again very helpful in opening the well-stocked archives and was also more than happy to assist. Greg Goodell, also a ranger

at the park, provided a number of important images. Dan Vermilya, a ranger at Eisenhower Historic Site, provided a few key images of Ike. Finally, Andrew Dalton, executive director of the Adams County Historical Society, provided encouragement and permission to use a myriad of photos.

Finally, a special thanks to Chris Mackowski. The Emerging Civil War Series is his baby, and the books have helped thousands gain a meaningful knowledge of the seminal conflict in United States history. He has also been a wonderful colleague and supporter. This book could not have been produced without his abundant encouragement and expertise.

Battery H, 1st Ohio Artillery consisted of 123 men and six three-inch ordnance rifles. Posted on Cemetery Hill, they suffered three killed and four wounded. (cm)

PHOTO CREDITS:
Adams County Historical Society (achs); findagrave.com (fg); Friends of Mt. Moriah Cemetery (fommc); Gettysburg Guides (gg); Gettysburg National Military Park (gnmp); Gettysburg Presbyterian Church (gpc); Linda Gottfried (lg); Harper's Weekly (hw); Chris Mackowski (cm); Massachusettes Order of the Loyal Legion of the United States (mollus); National Park Service (nps); New York Times (nyt); Pennlive.com (pl); Dan Welch (dw) Wikimedia Commons (wc); Wikipedia (wp)

Foreword

BY DOUG DOUDS

Lincoln, cast here in bronze, recast the meaning of the war with his "few appropriate remarks." (cm)

President Lincoln was invited to make "a few appropriate remarks" to help dedicate the Soldiers National Cemetery at Gettysburg. It is often supposed by title alone that his Gettysburg Address followed the great Union military victory at Gettysburg, the Civil War's bloodiest battle. However, after the battle of Gettysburg but before Lincoln's address, the most significant Union defeat in the Western Theater occurred at Chickamauga and produced the war's second-bloodiest battlefield. The defeat tarnished the luster of triple, summer Union victories at Gettysburg, Tullahoma, and Vicksburg. Again, the war's outcome and the fate of the Republic were uncertain.

Lincoln's remarks followed Edward Everett, the keynote speaker at the November 19, 1863, dedication. As Everett's last words faded, the crowd cheered. A choir of men sang an ode. Then, Abraham Lincoln rose, stepped forward, and began his Gettysburg Address. Lincoln delivered his 272 words in 10 sentences in just over two minutes.

Although Lincoln physically wore his prized stove-piped hat that day, he rhetorically wore three hats in his remarks. The three hats corresponded to three roles he occupied simultaneously: citizen, commander-in-chief, and president of the United States. He invited the audience to time travel with him and glimpse the battle of Gettysburg, the American Civil War, and the United States through the lenses associated with each of those roles.

As a U.S. citizen, Lincoln goes back in time, *"four score and seven years ago."* The eighty-seven years he refers to does not take the audience back to the Constitution, a compromise document that included slavery in the language of "other persons"—a compromise necessary to articulate the workings of the fledgling nation, but which also lit the fuze that seventy-three years later erupted into the Civil War. Rather, Lincoln's journey takes the audience back in time to the Declaration of Independence and reminds us of our nation's founding values: *"all men"*—all people— *"are created equal."*

As the commander-in-chief, he is present in the moment as he stands amid the cemetery, scans the freshly dug graves, and looks to his right to see the last remaining wounded soldiers still recovering in field hospitals who have come to the dedication. As the commander-in-chief, he sees the great cost in human lives and recognizes the fallen by saying, *"it is altogether fitting and proper that we should do this,"* that we should honor those who have given *"the last full measure of devotion."*

As the president of the United States, Lincoln steps into the future and asks for increased resolve that *"these men not have died in vain."* Then, he does something remarkable as he stands on the physical high ground of Cemetery Hill: he puts the nation on a moral high ground for all the world to see *"that government of the people, by the people, for the people shall not perish from the earth."*

How does Lincoln make time travel happen in just over two minutes? His secret is that he anchors that travel by using the word *"here"* nine times. On that high ground—Cemetery Hill, in Gettysburg—and from that moment two years into the national bloodletting that was the Civil War, Lincoln offers that from *here*, you can look back and see where we have been. From *here*, you can see our present condition. From here, we can propel ourselves into the future.

To emphasize that our national journey is a collective one of "we the people," Lincoln deliberately choses the language of leadership and inclusivity. Fifteen times, he invokes the collective pronouns of *"we," "us,"* and *"our."* What is more, because he uses language like "the great task remaining" and the "unfinished work," his words still speak to us. Today's headlines remind us that the Union is far from perfect and that "the task" and "work" are all around us.

Lincoln ended by saying that *"the world will little note, nor long remember what we say here, but it can never forget what they did here."* Yet, as a Licensed Battlefield Guide at Gettysburg, I have given tours to people from around the world and can attest that most have little idea "what they did here." However, I am always humbled and inspired when people of all ages visit where Lincoln gave his address in the Gettysburg Soldiers National Cemetery. It is common that standing "here" reveals that they know every word that Lincoln spoke on that November day. It is then that I am reminded that this notion of government of, by, and for the people—if it does not exist here, it does not exist anywhere.

The day after the event, Edward Everett wrote Lincoln to say, "I should be glad, if I could flatter myself that I came as near to the central idea of the occasion, in two hours as you did in two minutes." Even then, he knew that Lincoln's remarks sought a more elevated and timeless destination. By not mentioning Union, slavery, or even Gettysburg by name, Lincoln's words transcended space and time. While "our fathers brought forth on this on this continent a new nation conceived in liberty," and the Civil War was "testing whether that nation … so conceived and dedicated could long endure," Lincoln connected the nation's founding values of liberty and freedom with the human condition across the earth and for all time.

My hope for you, having invested in this book, is that reading it will give you a better understanding of what Lincoln said there, what they did there, and that both still matter today.

COLONEL DOUG DOUDS, *USMC (Ret.), is a professor at the U.S. Army War College and a Gettysburg Licensed Battlefield Guide. An avid historian, he enjoys hosting leadership education tours (staff rides) of Civil War battlefields.*

Four score and seven years ago our fathers brought forth on this continent, a new nation, conceived in Liberty, and dedicated to the proposition that all men are created equal.

Now we are engaged in a great civil war, testing whether that nation, or any nation so conceived and so dedicated, can long endure. We are met on a great battle-field of that war. We have come to dedicate a portion of that field, as a final resting place for those who here gave their lives that that nation might live. It is altogether fitting and proper that we should do this.

But, in a larger sense, we can not dedicate—we can not consecrate—we can not hallow—this ground. The brave men, living and dead, who struggled here, have consecrated it, far above our poor power to add or detract. The world will little note, nor long remember what we say here, but it can never forget what they did here. It is for us the living, rather, to be dedicated here to the unfinished work which they who fought here have thus far so nobly advanced. It is rather for us to be here dedicated to the great task remaining before us—that from these honored dead we take increased devotion to that cause for which they gave the last full measure of devotion—that we here highly resolve that these dead shall not have died in vain—that this nation, under God, shall have a new birth of freedom—and that government of the people, by the people, for the people, shall not perish from the earth.

—*Abraham Lincoln*
November 19, 1863

Prologue

Abraham Lincoln slowly rose from his seat on the platform to share a few appropriate words with the ghosts of the dead and the moans of the wounded still lingering in the air. Lincoln's address at the dedication of what would become the National Cemetery at Gettysburg on November 19, 1863, has endured generations, but can only truly be appreciated when placed in the context of the time and place those words were delivered: four months and 16 days after the horrific battle at Gettysburg.

The bloody three-day battle ended as the sun slipped beyond the horizon on July 3. A variety of thoughts occupied the living—gratitude for surviving, worry about the future, and concern for missing comrades. Survivors witnessed both town and field littered with thousands of dead and wounded, shading their worry and concern with despair.

The losses were astronomical. The Union army lost 23,055; the Confederate army, 23,231. No battle in the Civil War—before or after—claimed so many lives. The numbers of dead are open to debate, but have been estimated at almost 8,000. This number does not include the thousands—perhaps as many as 4,000—who died from wounds after the battle ended. The dead required burying, but they were only second in priority to the 22,000 wounded dotting the fields, who needed medical attention.

North and South Carolina troops charged across these open fields on the afternoon of July 1 to attack the Union troops making a last stand in front of the Lutheran Theological Seminary. These fields were filled with dead and wounded Union and Confederate troops. (lg)

That any men survived is a miracle. Staff officer, Lt. Frank Haskell rode along Culp's Hill on July 6 and observed:

Thirty-five-year-old Capt. Frank Haskell served as an aide-de-camp to Gen. John Gibbon. The Dartmouth University graduate, attorney, and Wisconsin-native wrote a seminal book on his Gettysburg experience. He later commanded a regiment and was killed at the battle of Cold Harbor. (mollus)

the trees were almost literally peeled, from the ground up some fifteen or twenty feet, so thick upon them were the scars the bullets had made. Upon a single tree, not over a foot and a half in diameter, I actually counted as many as two hundred and fifty bullet marks. The ground was covered by the little twigs that had been cut off by the hailstorm of lead.

Thomas Knox also ventured out to Culp's Hill on the same day as Lt. Haskell and reported in the New York Herald: "The storm of bullets must have been as thick as hailstones in an ordinary storm. How a man could exist in it and come out unhurt is difficult to imagine."

Jacob Hoke, a civilian from Chambersburg, Pennsylvania, roamed the fields several days after the battle and noted, "paper, envelopes, bits of letters, shreds of clothing, pieces of photographs, muskets, bayonets, ramrods, knapsacks, haversacks, caps, old shoes and blankets, and many other articles were scattered everywhere. The trees were riddled with balls. . . . Long trenches, heaped over with fresh earth, told where tens, twenties and fifties of rebels were

The intensity of battle was easily observed on Culp's Hill, which saw fighting on the second and third days of the battle. (loc)

interred."

The dead, no matter their uniform or beliefs, looked the same. The 90-degree heat quickly triggered rigor mortis, causing the corpses to take on grotesque poses. Faces turned black in the heat and swelled into ghastly proportions. In addition, the stench emanating from the dead—a sickening smell magnified by the thousands. Add to that the scent of thousands of unwashed bodies mixed with the urine and feces strewn upon the battlefield, and you have a scene out of hell.

The excessive heat caused rigor mortis to set in fairly quickly. Alabamians from Law's Brigade who fell in the Slaughter Pen are represented in this photo. (gnmp)

Private John Haley of the 17th Maine Infantry was on the picket line on the evening of July 3 near Emmitsburg Road:

> *The dead lay everywhere, and although not a half day has passed since they died, the stench is so great that we can neither eat, drink, nor sleep. Decomposition commences as soon as life is extinct. . . . No tongue can depict the carnage, and I cannot make it seem real: men's heads blown off or split open; horrible gashes cut; some split from the top of the head to the extremities, as butchers split beef.*

Vermont Private Wilbur Fisk took in the battlefield near his unit on July 5:

> *The rebel dead and ours lay thickly together, their thirst for blood forever quenched. Their bodies were swollen, black and hideously unnatural. Their eyes glared from their sockets, their tongues protruded from their mouths, and in almost every case, clots of blood and mangled flesh showed how they had died, and rendered a sight ghastly beyond description. . . . I turned away from the heart-sickening sight, willing to forego gratifying my curiosity rather than dwell upon the horrors of that battle-field. I thought I had become hardened*

Photographer Timothy O'Sullivan, one of Alexander Gardner's assistants, captioned this photo, "A harvest of Death." It may show the I Corps dead after the first day's action. (loc)

to almost anything, but *I cannot say I ever wish to see another sight like that I saw on the battle-field of Gettysburg.*

J. Howard Wert, who later served as a lieutenant in the 209th Pennsylvania, left his home near Gettysburg and noted,

Festering corpses at every step; some, still unburied, some, hastily and rudely buried with so little of earth upon them that the appearance presented was almost as repulsive as where no attempt at burial had been made. . . The dead

Photographer Alexander Gardner and his staff descended on Gettysburg soon after the battle. His mobile processing lab wagon can be seen in the background. (gnmp)

were everywhere. In some cases, nothing but a few mutilated fragments and pieces of flesh were left of what had been so late a human being following his flag to death or victory.

And it got worse. Swarms of flies descended, covering dead bodies with eggs hatching to form wiggling maggots consuming the rotting flesh. Other insects appeared and feasted on the maggots. John Campbell noted, "every fence and bush was black with flies, but not a crow or buzzard [was] to be seen anywhere." Perhaps most horrible of all were the mammals roaming the battlefield. The chief culprit was the wild pigs who set upon the dead and the not so dead with ravenous appetites. John Wert recalled, "swine were found reveling in the remains [of a corpse] in a manner horrible to contemplate." Several wounded soldiers recounted their experiences trying to fend off these hungry creatures with swords, sticks, and guns.

J. Howard Wert was a 21-year-old school teacher who had recently graduated from Pennsylvania College when the war broke out. During the Gettysburg campaign, he scouted and guided for the Army of the Potomac. He officially joined the army in 1864. (achs)

Initial Burying of the Dead

CHAPTER ONE
July 1-8, 1863

In the turmoil of combat, dead bodies splayed in the no-man's land between two armies had little chance for burial, but even those behind the lines were often left unburied because the men were exhausted or were ordered to march toward the Potomac River. Dead bodies render a universally revolting stench and also create a potential for the spread of disease. Burial as quickly as possible became a priority.

Men fought for each other, cared for each other, and suffered when a comrade perished. Whenever possible, soldiers scoured the battlefield looking for a comrade and when found, provided a loving burial. These graves were dug deep, lined with blankets or knapsacks, the body carefully lowered into the hole and then covered again with blankets or other accoutrements. Placing a headboard on the grave was the last step in the process.

This careful burial was rare, however. The task of tending to so many bodies was overwhelming, and most were thrown unceremoniously into shallow graves. This was especially true for Confederate dead. A soldier on burial detail bemoaned the fact the dead "were on every side of us. . . . They were so many it seemed a gigantic task." Army commander General George Meade reported his men buried 2,890 Confederates. This number does not include the considerable number buried by members of

The area of the Devil's Den/Houck's Ridge was the scene of intense fighting on the afternoon of July 2. It was ultimately captured by the Confederates, but had little strategic value. (lg)

Philadelphian George
Meade was a West Pointer
whose distinguished career
as brigade, division, and
corps commander led to his
elevation as commander of
the Army of the Potomac a
mere three days before the
battle. He would continue
commanding the army
through the end of the war. (loc)

Marsena Patrick was a West
Point graduate who left the
military to become a railroad
president, successful farmer,
and college president. He
rejoined the army at the
outbreak of the war and
rose to the rank of brigadier
general, commanding a
brigade at the battle of
Antietam. He served the
remainder of the war as
provost marshal of the army.
(loc)

the XI and XII Corps and those interred by their comrades prior to leaving the battlefield. He did not supply the number of his own men buried but the number would have approached that of Confederates placed in the ground. Thousands of fallen remained and became the job of the army's provost marshal, Brig. Gen. Marsena Patrick, who mobilized all his resources to get the job done.

Four groups were pressed into service to bury the dead: soldiers, the provost marshal, Confederate prisoners, and civilians. The paltry amount of available manpower made the job near impossible. Patrick threw up his hands during a meeting with Gen. Meade on July 5 and admitted he was having difficulty completing the immense task. He authorized some of his officers to go into town to organize burial parties, but they could find few takers. He later wrote, "Had a great deal of difficulty in getting hold of some respectable parties to do anything with, the people being nearly all Copperheads [Southern sympathizers]. In desperation, Gen. Patrick convened a meeting of the town's leading citizens at attorney David Wills's office and they identified Samuel Herbst as just the man for the job.

The provost marshal continued burying the dead and enlisting civilian help. A reader of the *Adams County Sentinel* during the week after the battle would have come across this advertisement:

To All Citizens
Men, Horses and Wagons wanted immediately, to bury the dead and to cleanse our streets, in such a thorough way as to guard against pestilence. Every good citizen can be of use by reporting himself, at once, to Capt. W.W. Smith, acting Provost Marshal, office, N.E. corner, Centre Square.

The advertisement attracted only a few volunteers, but several others were pressed into duty when found illegally collecting guns and accoutrements from the battlefield and even rifling the dead's pockets.

The job of burying the dead was so immense a visitor to the battlefield seven days after the end of the conflict observed many Confederate corpses still lying about, decomposing rapidly. Indeed, the provost marshal details could bury but 367 Confederate dead and 100 horses between July 8 and 12. The burial of Confederate dead extended well into July.

Burial crews roamed the battlefield to locate and quickly bury the dead. These corpses were probably located near the base of the Round Tops. (loc)

The men assigned to burial details avoided any direct contact with the corpses. William Baird of the 6th Michigan Cavalry explained it was a "very trying job as they had become much decomposed" and Bay Stater Robert Carter described the ghastly details of dead "so far decomposed . . . as they slid into the trenches, broke apart, to the horror and disgust of the whole party, and the stench still lingers in our nostrils." The men devised a variety of methods to get the bodies to the burial sites. Baird and his comrades used a "stretcher . . . made of two poles sixteen feet long with a strip of canvass sowed [sic] to them in the middle long enough to carry a man." Upon reaching a corpse, two men would lay the rails upwind from the body and a third used

The bodies of comrades were often buried with some form of identification. The bodies of these South Carolinians had headboards to reveal their identity. (gnmp)

a pike to push the body onto the canvas.

Men dug a variety of graves. According to Alanson Haines of the 15th New Jersey Infantry, "a grave was dug beside where the body lay, and it was merely turned over into the narrow pit. Sometimes long trenches were dug, and in single lines, with head to foot, one corpse after another was laid in; then the earth was thrown back, making a long ridge of fresh ground."

Sgt. Thomas Meyer of the 148th Pennsylvania Infantry explained another way of disposing of the bodies:

Some of the men buried the dead thus laid in rows; a shallow grave about a foot deep, [was dug] against the first man in a row and he was then laid down into it; a similar grave was dug where he had lain. The ground thus dug up served to cover the first man, and the second was laid in the trench, and so on, so the ground was handled only once. This was the regular form of burial on our battlefields. It is the most rapid, and is known as trench burial and is employed where time for work is limited.

Burial details after the battle were primarily interested in getting the corpses into the ground as soon as possible. They lined the bodies in rows, dug trenches, and deposited the bodies in them. (loc)

After the armies left Gettysburg, the immense task of burying the dead became more difficult. The provost marshal resorted to an ad in the newspaper to attract volunteers, but there were few takers. (gnmp)

To all Citizens,

Men, Horses and Wagons wanted immediately, to bury the dead and to cleanse our streets, in such a thorough way as to guard against a pestilence. Every good citizen can be of use by reporting himself, at once, to Capt. W. W. SMITH, acting Provost Marshal, Office, N. E. corner Centre Square.

Many of the dead were shipped home to be buried close to their loved one. A J. M. Fisher paid the Adams Express Company to transport a corpse to Delaware. (gnmp)

There was no time for mourning or prayer. Robert Carter lamented the fact "most of them were tumbled in just as they fell, with not a prayer, eulogy or tear to distinguish them from so many animals."

Coping with the overwhelming number of dead forced the grave-diggers to take shortcuts. Nurse Jane Boswell Moore volunteered her services at a Union II Corps hospital and with some free time on July 26, she decided to roam the battlefield at the site of Pickett's Charge:

> We walk along the low stone wall or breastworks . . . the hillocks of graves—[and] the little forest of headboards scattered everywhere. . . . Oh how they [the Confederates] must have struggled along that wall, where coats, hats, canteens and guns are so thickly strewn, beyond it two immense trenches filled with rebel dead, and surrounded with gray caps, attest the cost to them. The earth is scarcely thrown over them, and the skulls with ghastly grinning teeth appear, now that the few spadesful of earth are washed away.

About a month later, Baltimore resident Ambrose Emory also wandered the battlefield and noted near Little Round Top "men not half buried. It may be a skull, an arm, a leg protruding from the ground, barely in many instances covered over."

Although the Union dead were reburied in the Soldiers' Cemetery, the Confederate dead remained in the fields until the 1870's when thousands were sent south to be buried in Confederate sections of cemeteries. (loc)

GETTYSBURG BATTLE FIELD

Comrades felt compelled to mark the bodies or graves with the names of the fallen, hence Moore's description of the "forest of headboards" described above. These belonged to fallen Union soldiers and helped loved ones find their bodies. They also assisted in identifying the bodies as they were removed to the new Soldiers' Cemetery. A grave-digging New Jersey soldier recalled, "whenever names could be ascertained, each grave was marked by a head-board, with name and regiment of the dead soldier."

New Hampshire resident Joseph Foster perused the battlefield about two weeks after the battle. He noted,

1932

1863

DANIEL ALEXANDER SKELLY

Daniel Skelly was only a teenager when the armies arrived at Gettysburg.
He worked as a clerk at a Gettysburg dry goods store when not in school. His observations during the time of the battle were published in 1932 as *A Boy's Experience During the Battle of Gettysburg*. He died later that year at the age of 87. (achs)

> *The saddest marks are the graves of those killed. They are in all direction, sometimes singly, sometimes in little groups of from 3 to 12. Some are marked with a board, carefully cut with the name and regiment, others have merely a stick with the initials scratched on it, and still others have no mark whatever to show who sleeps there. The graves are generally very hastily dug not more than 18 inches deep, and coffins of course are out of the question.*

The retreating Confederates felt the same urge to identify fallen brothers in arms. Daniel Skelly, a Gettysburg resident observed a curious sight near Devil's Den:

twenty-six Confederate officers, ranking from colonel to lieutenants, laid side by side in a row for burial. At the head of each was a board giving their names, ranks, and commands to which they belonged. . . . They had evidently been prepared for burial by their Confederate companions before they had fallen back, so that their identity would be preserved, and they would receive a respectable burial.

In addition to the ghastly numbers of men killed, at least 3,000 horses and mules died during the battle. It was an equally horrific sight to see their carcasses littering the landscape. Many other wounded animals wandered the fields until rounded up and brought to a field near Rock Creek where they were shot. These animals were buried or burned.

The men deployed to bury the dead were exposed to sights they would never forget, but most recalled the stench most vividly. Sgt. Meyer commented, "stench on the battlefield was something indescribable, it would come up as if in waives and when at its worst the breath would stop in the throat; the lungs could not take it in, and a sense of suffocation would be experienced." Officers liberally distributed whiskey to dull their men's senses.

The unusual field of boulders populating Devil's Den was captured by Brig. Gen. George "Rock" Benning's Georgia brigade (First Corps) after bitter combat with J. H. Hobart Ward's brigade (III Corps) on the afternoon of July 2. (loc)

Visitors to the battlefield were repulsed by the smells and sights. It was especially horrible in the fields north and west where the first day's fighting occurred. Because they were behind Lee's lines, most of the dead were not buried until after Lee pulled away from Gettysburg on the evening of July 4 "The atmosphere is truly horrible," one woman wrote, "and camphor and smelling salts are prime necessities for most persons, certainly the ladies."

The Need for a Cemetery

CHAPTER TWO

July 9-August 25, 1863

As the first invaders of Gettysburg retreated, three more waves arrived. Most important were the medical personnel to help care for the thousands of wounded wedged into warehouses, churches, businesses, and private homes. Secondly, family members swept the battlefield to retrieve bodies of their loved ones or in better circumstances visit them in hospitals. Curiosity seekers and collectors formed the third group, wandering the battlefield, collecting guns and accoutrements, and gazing at the macabre sights. The provost marshal soon put an end to this practice.

The formation of the national cemetery revolves around forty-six-year-old Pennsylvania Governor Andrew Curtin. He was the right person for a difficult job. When the Confederate army approached Pennsylvania, Curtin recruited militia and effectively mobilized them, sent directives about securing goods and property to merchants and bankers, and was a steadying force during a very stressful period. In the aftermath of the battle, Curtin was embroiled in dealing with the fading invasion of his state and faced a difficult re-election campaign, so his visit to Gettysburg was delayed. Instead of arriving himself, he did something even better— he mobilized a militia unit to Gettysburg to assist the beleaguered town.

The site of the original Adams County Court House, Gettysburg's Square or Diamond has been the center of the town's activities for more than 150 years. (lg)

After the armies left the area, the provost marshal and his men were tasked with gathering supplies from the battlefield, warding off souvenir hunters, and keeping the peace. The provost marshal's office was located on the northeast corner of the Diamond, next to what is now the Gettysburg Hotel. This is a modern photograph of the building. (lg)

Andrew Gregg Curtin, the wartime governor of Pennsylvania, served in that capacity from 1861-1867. He effectively prepared his state for Robert E. Lee's invasion and made the wise decision of appointing attorney David Wills as his agent. His strong support of Abraham Lincoln was one of the reasons why the president journeyed to Gettysburg. (loc)

The 36th Pennsylvania Volunteer Militia arrived in Gettysburg on July 9, 1863, after a difficult 35-mile march. Commander, Col. H. C. Alleman, appointed Military Governor of Gettysburg and its surrounding fields, and his men completed a myriad of tasks, including gathering the wounded still in the fields, burying men and horses, and collecting federal property littering the battlefield in large quantities. The regiment made its camp on Cemetery Hill, just across Baltimore Pike from the Evergreen Cemetery.

The citizens of Gettysburg became increasingly concerned about family members digging up the battlefield to claim their loved ones' bodies and agitated Col. Alleman to terminate the practice. At the end of July, he issued orders preventing graves from being opened during the hot months of August and September. A letter published in the August 25, 1863, edition of the *Adams Sentinel* thanked Alleman because continued disinterment would have "produced wide-spread sickness and distress. Our atmosphere was that of a charnel house."

Curtin finally arrived in Gettysburg on the afternoon of July 10. A newspaper article explained Curtin's mission as giving "his personal attention to the care of the wounded men in the hospitals in that vicinity." The governor was unprepared for the sights and smells of the battlefield and quickly broadened his scope of understanding. Interactions

The debris of battle remained for weeks after the battle. Among the most egregious smells were those emanating from the dead horses and mules that littered the battlefield. These were either buried or hauled to Culp's Hill, where they were burned. (loc)

with civilians made it clear that Curtin needed to deal with the effect of the battle on the town and its residents. He was also mindful of a recent Pennsylvania law requiring the state to care for its war wounded and burial of its dead. The federal government had mobilized to care for the wounded, so his efforts must be concentrated on other issues, such as the disposition of the dead.

Andrew Curtin was in his first term as Pennsylvania's governor and like President Lincoln, was unsure of his prospects for re-election. He too had embraced the newly formed Republican Party's ideology and ran under its banner. He actively supported the war effort, but the strain caused a series of nervous breakdowns forcing Secretary of State Eli Slifer to step in to serve in his stead. Curtin was back to work during the Gettysburg Campaign and its aftermath taxed the governor. But he rose to the task, effectively guiding the town and the state through this very difficult period.

Curtin realized something needed to be done immediately to prevent further deterioration of the bodies and headboards. One observer explained the graves were everywhere, "in cornfields, in meadows, in gardens, by the way-side, and in the public road, buried hastily where they fell, and others in long rows, with a piece of box lid or board of any kind, with the name of the person and the day he died written with lead pencil, ink, or whatever they had to make a mark with." The writing on the headboards was becoming illegible even a few weeks after the battle, endangering

Col. H. C. Alleman commanded the 36th Regiment Pennsylvania Volunteer Militia. After the battle, he was appointed to serve as military governor of Gettysburg and the battleground district by Maj. Gen. Darius Couch, commander of the Department of the Susquehanna. (loc)

the possibility of ascertaining the identity of the soldier who had given his last full measure.

By his side during most of the governor's visit was thirty-two-year-old David Wills. Wills was a successful and aggressive attorney who lived in a stately home on the southeast corner of the Gettysburg Diamond or Square. His arrival in Gettysburg a mere nine years earlier gave testament to his personality, knowledge, and hard work. He was born on a farm near Bendersville, about ten miles north of Gettysburg, but his father abandoned life on the land and moved the family to Gettysburg when David was 13 years old. Wills later graduated from Pennsylvania College and moved south to Cahaba, Alabama, serving as the principal of the town's academy. He also taught some classes. Wills realized within a year his interests and talents lie outside of teaching, so he returned to Pennsylvania and studied law under the legendary Thaddeus Stevens. He was admitted to the Bar in 1854 and returned to Gettysburg where he established a law practice. A biographer described Wills as being "endowed with the attributes of the true pioneer, the strength of character, the fearless courage, the strong mental and physical characteristics, the indomitable will and tireless endurance."

Wills actively participated in civic affairs. Although a Republican in a strongly Democratic town, Wills was elected to the Town Council and rose to serve as its president. This speaks volumes about how fellow citizens felt about him, given the contentious interactions between members of the two political parties. He played a strong role in forming the Hanover Junction, Hanover, and Gettysburg Railroad, serving on the board as secretary. He was also elected as the first Superintendent of Adams County Schools in 1854 and for the next couple of years worked tirelessly to create an effective system of public education. He oversaw 137 schools taught by 156 chronically underpaid teachers with an enrollment of 8,157. He received $300 a year for this part-time engagement.

By the summer of 1863, Wills was married to the former Catherine Jane Smyser and was the father of three children with a fourth on the way.

Gov. Curtin may have seen a very special and unusual man in David Wills, who had a reputation of getting along with others to accomplish complex tasks. He also appreciated Wills' prominent standing in Adams County's Republican Party. Before Curtin departed Gettysburg, he appointed Wills as his "agent" in matters relating to Pennsylvania's dead soldiers. The editor of the *Adams County Sentinel*, who also happened to be Wills's neighbor, wrote in the July 28, 1863, edition that Wills would be responsible for the "removal of all Pennsylvanians killed in the late battles, furnishing transportation for the body and one attendant at the expense of the State." This statement echoed an earlier one in the *Harrisburg Daily Telegraph* on July 20, 1863, informing its readers that "every arrangement has been made at Gettysburg by Governor Curtin, for the removal, on application to David Wills, residing there, of the bodies of Pennsylvanians killed in the late battle."

Sending a body home was probably the easy part of the many steps preceding this end. Wills

The 29-acre Evergreen Cemetery was established in 1853 by a group of community leaders. Its iconic gatehouse continues to stand guard over the main entrance on East Cemetery Hill. (loc)

David Wills was a successful 32-year-old attorney who lived in a stately home on the Diamond. His close association with Governor Curtin and his "go-getter" approach caused him to be named Pennsylvania's agent in Gettysburg. This photo was taken when Wills was in his early 20s. (achs)

Catherine Jane Smyser married David Wills in 1856. The daughter of a wealthy family from York County, she may have helped Wills establish his successful law practice in Gettysburg. This photo was probably taken when Catherine was in her early 20s. (achs)

first needed to locate the grave, hire undertakers to exhume the body, and then secure a coffin. The 1,000 Pennsylvanians killed at Gettysburg made this a daunting task. He was charged with determining the fate of the 1,300 listed as missing or captured and ensuring the adequate care of the 4,000 wounded Keystone State soldiers. Wills organized an effective supply chain for coffin production that put many Gettysburg residents to work. The *Adams County Sentinel* reported on July 21, 1863, that local craftsmen had already fashioned 600-700 coffins. There was also the never-ending correspondence from family members inquiring about the missing or wounded. Wills responded to each and every message by hand.

The case of W.H.H. Coates of the 121st Pennsylvania Volunteers illustrates the enormity of the task. Upon confirming that Coates was not with the army, Wills checked the records of wounded in various hospitals, but this proved fruitless. He then traveled to the I Corps hospital and spoke with a couple of Coates's comrades who did not believe he was wounded. Trying to ascertain this soldier's whereabouts took him several days, so one can imagine how overwhelmed he must have been as he received dozens of requests to locate other soldiers. Wills admitted being an agent of the state was "an undertaking of much greater magnitude than [I] contemplated." Quitting was not in Wills's constitution and he forged on, spending countless hours on his responsibilities. He could never get a reprieve from the terrible battle. His house became a hospital and one officer recalled the "house was full of wounded."

State agents from other states also engaged in extensive mapping efforts to document the location of their dead. Dr. Theodore Dimon of New York assumed one such effort. He wrote to New York State's General Agent, John Seymour, on July 16, 1863: "In regard to our dead, I would say that I made a map, enlarged from the county map of the whole district of the battle-field, and procured a careful record of the names and places of burial

of our dead soldiers, referring to the map for the places of burial. This record contains all whose remains can be identified. The headboards were also marked distinctly whenever necessary. This map and record are presented with this report."

John Bachelder, who would emerge as the most influential person in the early development of the battlefield, arrived at Gettysburg soon after the battle to document the battlefield and the events occurring there. He proposed to Gov. Curtin on August 10, 1863:

Like many 19th century towns, Gettysburg's Diamond, or Square, dominated the center of town. A 120-foot flagpole graced the center of the Diamond during the consecration cemetery. (achs)

> *I find that a large proportion of them [head-boards] were written with lead pencil and by the rains beating the fresh earth upon them have already become nearly effaced and before the coming autumn many will be entirely obliterated. Massachusetts sent a committee here to remark the names of her sons that had fallen in battle. . . . I visit every enclosure and take every name. I now propose to the Executives of different States for a fair compensation to good men to go with me and remark every name that may need it, and when necessary put up new headboards. The expense will be but a trifle. . . .*

Even a cursory scan of the hallowed battlefield dotted with fading headboards begged for immediate steps to more effectively bury the dead. The governors of most states appointed their own state agents to help with the dead and Wills worked with all of them.

Several prominent citizens claimed to have birthed the idea of a national cemetery to honor the Union dead. Prominent among this group was Theodore Dimon, a former army surgeon who was sent south to assist New York's agent, John Seymour, "for the relief of sick and wounded soldiers." Many relatives were pouring into Gettysburg soon after the battle to claim the remains of their loved ones. Dimon realized this was only practical for those who had the resources to accomplish this costly task. He also understood the impracticality of removing all the dead "to their former homes, and especially in the case of the more distant States." Dimon decided to assemble his counterparts from other states and approached David Wills, Pennsylvania's agent, with a request that he open his office to a meeting to present his idea for a national cemetery. Dimon later reported to New York Gov. Horatio Seymour,

> *I presented a proposition that a portion of the ground occupied by our line of battle on Cemetery Hill should be purchased for a permanent burial place for the soldiers of our army who lost their lives in this battle, or who died here of their wounds; and that their bodies be gathered from the fields in which they were interred and deposited in this burial place by regiments and States with proper marks designating their graves.*

Dimon noted in his journal that it "occurred to me as practicable to have a piece of ground purchased for a burial place on or near the battlefield, to which the dead bodies of all our soldiers should be removed and there buried by regiments and states and their graves permanently marked."

David Wills also reported on this meeting, but did not credit Dimon with organizing it, instead suggesting he called the meeting. In fact, he did not even acknowledge Dimon's presence at the meeting. Wills wrote to Gov. Curtin about the meeting: "Mr. Seymour is here on behalf of his Brother the Governor of New York to look after the wounded. . . ." Gettysburg National Park Service Historian Kathy Georg carefully reviewed the historical record and noted that Seymour had returned to New York, so he could not have been present at the meeting. She supported Dimon's claim that he represented New York at the conference. This was not an oversight and begs the question of why Wills would tell an untruth to Governor Curtin. Georg believes that Wills needed Curtin's support and the best way to get it was by noting the Governor's brother supported his idea. Georg went on to state, "Because Wills was less than truthful, then, in his July 24 letter to Governor Curtin, we can be more assured that the journal and letters of Theodore Dimon are correct, and that Dimon was the 'founder' of the National Cemetery concept at Gettysburg."

John Bachelder was 38 years old when he first visited the battlefield soon after the conclusion of the battle. He devoted his life to the study of the battle, inviting scores of veterans on both sides back to the battlefield to help mark the units and better understand what transpired. (gnmp)

Daniel Welch of the Gettysburg Foundation took a less definitive approach, noting, "The truth may lie somewhere between the Dimon and Wills accounts of that late July meeting. The sheer scope of the cleanup efforts at Gettysburg demanded the attention of many during the months following the battle. . . . Representatives for numerous other states, as well as civilian relief organizations and an army presence, all worked towards a common goal. Certainly, numerous ideas were proposed during this period by various parties invested in this work." We may never really know the answer, but even if Wills was not the father of the cemetery idea, it in

The Christian Commission established a warehouse at the John Schick store, which sat at the intersection of Baltimore Street and the Diamond. (lg)

no way minimizes the herculean task he undertook to sell the idea and see it through to fruition.

Eminent Lincoln scholar Frank Klement agreed: "Without Wills's perception, promotion, and planning there would have been no Gettysburg-based oration by Everett nor address by Lincoln." Wills probably understood the challenges associated with each state's agent working independently. This created a haphazard approach as some agents were more effective than others. As Pennsylvania's agent, Wills took the heat from farmers whose land remained dotted with inadequately buried men. The farmers were trying to achieve some normalcy and prepare for the next growing season, but the battle's aftermath conspired against their efforts. Dimon noted in his journal: "It seemed wrong to leave the soldier 'buried like a dead horse,' when in another year all marks of his grave would be obliterated by the owner of the soil." Andrew Cross of the Christian Commission of Pennsylvania also claimed at least partial credit for the idea of the cemetery, explaining he had "exchanged views [with Wills] about the desirability of transforming a portion of the battlefield into a cemetery and getting all of the eighteen states that had lost sons at Gettysburg to cooperate in the venture." He later worked with the press to drum up support for a cemetery for the fallen Union soldiers in an article appearing in the *Harrisburg Daily Telegraph* on July 29, 1863.

The Fight Over the National Cemetery's Location

CHAPTER THREE

July 24-August 25, 1863

Who arrived at the idea of a national cemetery is less important than the movement toward its establishment. David Wills began the process with a letter to Gov. Curtin dated July 24, 1863, written either the day of the meeting with the state agents or the day after the seminal meeting. He got right to the point of the letter: the "necessity of the purchase of a common burial ground for the dead, now only partially buried over miles of country around Gettysburg." Wills had a specific site in mind: "the elevated piece of ground on the Baltimore Turnpike opposite the [Evergreen] Cemetery." He described the property as the "place where our army had about 40 pieces of artillery . . . the point on which the desperate attack was made by the Louisiana Brigades. . . . It was the key to the whole line of our defenses—the apex of the triangular line of battle."

Wills went on to explain the land encompassed two lots of about eight acres: "three and a half owned by Mr. [Peter] Raffensperger and four and a half owned by Mr. [Edward] Menchy." Both agreed to sell their pieces at a price of $200 per acre. "This is not much out of the way and I think it should be secured at once and the project started." These two parcels lie adjacent to Baltimore Pike on what is now called East Cemetery Hill.

Wills continued the letter by providing a gruesome accounting of the situation: "Our dead

The iconic Evergreen Cemetery Gatehouse was built in 1855 to house the cemetery's office and the caretaker's quarters. General Oliver Howard, commander of the Union XI Corps, made the gatehouse his headquarters. (lg)

Forty-year-old David McConaughy was a prominent figure in Gettysburg prior to the battle. An attorney by trade, he immersed himself in bettering Gettysburg. (achs)

are lying on the fields unburied (that is, no grave being dug) with small portion of earth dug up alongside of the body and thrown over it. In many instances, arms and legs and sometimes heads protrude, and my attention has been directed to several places where the hogs were actually rooting out the bodies and devouring them." His plan was for "Pennsylvania to purchase the ground at once so as to furnish a place for the friends of those who are here seeking places for the permanent burial of their fallen ones to inter them at once and also be a place for the burial of hundreds who are dying in the hospitals." He believed, "The other states would certainly through their Legislatures in cooperation with our own Legislature contribute towards defraying the expenses." He ended the letter with: "You will please favor me with an early answer. If the matter is delayed I am afraid the owners of the land might be operated on by speculators."

This communication may have surprised Gov. Curtin. Just four days earlier, one of Curtin's aides outlined Wills's marching orders in a communication printed in the *Pennsylvania Daily Telegraph*: The idea was for the "removal, on application to David Wills, residing there, of the bodies of Pennsylvanians killed in the late battle. A map of the battle-field has been made, which shows the exact locality of every grave." The letter clearly indicates that Curtin was not envisioning a new cemetery, but he quickly embraced the idea and told Wills to begin the process of securing the necessary land.

Utilizing a state law, Curtin established a special corporation to oversee all phases in the development of a new National Soldiers' Cemetery. This approach included forming a Trustee Board comprised of a commissioner from each state who had lost sons at Gettysburg. Such a corporation could own and manage a cemetery without political interference. Each governor appointed his own representative.

The idea of a national cemetery whose costs were borne by all seventeen states must have been a comfort to Gov. Curtin, but he was blissfully unaware of a brewing second battle of Gettysburg that would consume hours of his time and create no small amount of anxiety. The day after Wills penned the letter recommending the creation of the new cemetery, Curtin received a letter from respected Gettysburg attorney, David McConaughy. Unlike Wills, McConaughy's Gettysburg roots were deep and distinguished and the two men often tangled in the courtroom and probably disliked each other. Unlike the affable Wills, McConaughy was thin skinned and liable to lash out at perceived slights through letters to the editor of local newspapers. Like Wills, McConaughy

As president of the Evergreen Cemetery Board, David McConaughy spent hours in his home and office, lobbying hard for the Soldiers' Cemetery to be located at Evergreen. He also began buying up land around the town to preserve the battlefield and formed the Gettysburg Battlefield Memorial Association. (lg)

took an active role in community-building, serving as a moving force in the formation of the local YMCA and the Evergreen Cemetery on Cemetery Hill, formed nine years earlier. McConaughy became the Cemetery's board president and took an active interest in its well-being and growth. McConaughy has also been called the father of the Gettysburg National Military Park because of his vision and actions in buying up important parts of the battlefield almost as soon as the battle ended. Despite residing in the same small town, it appears Wills and McConaughy never joined forces in the same organizations.

As board president of the Evergreen Cemetery, McConaughy worried about the cemetery's tenuous finances. The battle created even more daunting problems. The *Adams Sentinel* reported, "The once beautiful 'Evergreen Cemetery' now presents a sad appearance. The ground . . . was literally strewed with shot and shell; a few tombstones erected over the remains of beloved relations were thrown from their positions or broken into fragments; graves were turned up by ploughing shot, and tasteful railings and other ornamental work around the lots were somewhat shattered." It would take money, and a lot of it, to help the cemetery return to its former beauty and gain a firm financial footing.

McConaughy had a plan. As early as June 24, 1862, over a year before the battle of Gettysburg, he envisioned a section of his Evergreen Cemetery devoted to the war dead. He wrote a letter to the editor of the *Adams Sentinel*:

> *Let there be a selection made of an eligible site and commodious ground in Ever Green Cemetery, and in the center let there be erected a handsome and imposing shaft of marble, around which will be interred the remains, and upon which shall be inscribed the names of all the glorious dead. . . . Let each grave be indicated by a small headstone.*

Now with an army of dead men crudely buried around the battlefield, McConaughy expanded his vision. A couple of soldiers from the area were already interred there, so it made sense to include the thousands of newly deceased in the cemetery. McConaughy realized his cemetery was inadequate to accommodate all of the newcomers so he did what Wills feared—approached Menchy and Raffensperger with offers to purchase their land. They gladly accepted, despite their word to Wills. McConaughy's July 25, 1863, letter to Gov. Curtin was straightforward:

> *I have purchased & now hold all the land upon Cemetery Hill which encircles the Ever Green Cemetery Ground, & which was occupied by the Artillery. . . . In doing so I have had two purposes, viz. to enlarge the area of our Cemetery, of which I am the President and (2d) to secure so as to be held in perpetuity, the most interesting portions of this illustrious Battlefield.*

The letter went on to explain he was purchasing other pieces of important battlefield land. He proposed a "public offer" to "patriotic citizens of our state" to help defray the cost of the battlefield land he was purchasing. McConaughy also informed the governor, "We have already buried nearly one hundred, at a cost (for ground & burial) of $5 each;

and we have abundant room for all who fell here, or have died since the battles." He also intended to "enter into arrangements with our state and with all the other loyal states, to bury the dead in such manner as shall be most agreeable to them & to arrange our grounds accordingly." Because the soldiers would be interred within the existing Evergreen Cemetery, McConaughy proposed a large "noble National Monument in memory of the battles & dead . . . similar to the Washington monument." McConaughy's idea was buoyed on July 23, 1863, when the Boston, Massachusetts, City Council began considering the purchase a lot in the "beautiful rural cemetery belonging to the city of Gettysburg" to bury its dead.

Although McConaughy purchased the land Wills coveted on the east side of Baltimore Pike, the Menchy's holdings would allow the Evergreen Cemetery to expand across the Pike and down the hill toward the town. McConaughy also purchased a portion of the Benner property between Taneytown Pike and Menchy's property. He now owned most of the land between Baltimore Pike and Taneytown Pike—the area partially encompassing the future Soldiers' National Cemetery.

The unburied bodies carried health risks, and many of the corpses were being eaten by wild pigs and other scavengers. (loc)

Gov. Curtin surely responded to McConaughy's letter, but the communication has not been found. It probably informed McConaughy of Wills's plan and may have asked him to call a meeting with him. Wills continued pushing the governor to allow him to purchase land for the national cemetery. He telegraphed Curtin on July 29, 1863, "Please advise me immediately by telegraph in reference to the contents of my letter Saturday. Shall I buy the land? There is an offer for it. I fear I cannot hold the owners longer without a promise of purchase."

McConaughy may have known Wills was lobbying Curtin, for on the morning of July 29, 1863, he quickly penned his own telegram to Gov. Curtin: "Will you say to Mr. Wills not to purchase land today for burial of our soldiers. I will come to see you this PM on the subject."

As can be expected, Wills was outraged by this turn of events. His vision for a national cemetery had been embraced by most of the state agents and was now in jeopardy. He lashed out at McConaughy, calling him a speculator. Wills paid a visit to Mr. Raffensperger and his wife while McConaughy was still in Harrisburg and implored them to break the verbal agreement with McConaughy. The latter recounted Wills's conversation with the Raffenspegers: "that I had bought not for a public but for a private purpose & for speculation. By these representations (utterly without foundation) he induced them to promise to sell to him." When McConaughy learned of these actions, he confronted the Raffenspergers and "insisted on my rights and explained to their satisfaction, and ratified our contract by writing under seal."

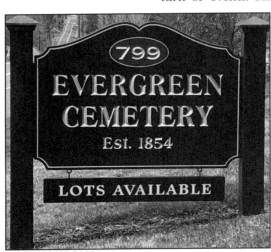

The location of the Soldiers' Cemetery pitted two influential Gettysburg attorneys against each other. Despite losing the battle to house the new cemetery, the 29-acre Evergreen Cemetery is the burial place of a veritable "who's who" of Gettysburg and Adams County. (lg)

Rebuffed in his efforts to foil McConaughy's land purchase, Wills played his ace. He suspected Curtin would favor a national effort to defray expenses, assuming all the states participated. Wills began calling meetings with the state agents at the end of July to garner support and telegraphed Gov. Curtin on July 31, 1863: "There is no doubt all the states will unite if a national exclusive burial ground for soldiers [is formed]. Eight have been consulted and some officially adopt the place . . . They oppose the plan being made use of for advancement of local enterprise and expense of the public. The project . . . meets with disfavor." Wills followed up with another telegram on August 3, 1863, informing the governor of several meetings held earlier that day. "The conclusion that the representatives from other states arrived at, was, that it must be independent of local influences & control. Second, that the Cemetery Hill is the best location if it can be secured." He ended the communication by indicating the meetings with McConaughy were fruitless: "The Conferences with him have not resulted in securing a transfer of the ground."

Wills continued playing the state agent card by sending telegrams on August 1 to each of the seventeen governors whose troops had fought and died at Gettysburg. "By authority of Governor Curtin, I am buying ground on or near Cemetery Hill in trust for a cemetery for the burial of the soldiers who fell here in the defense of the Union." He requested their cooperation with, and support of, this venture. He asked each governor to "signify your assent to Governor Curtin or myself and details [will] be arranged afterwards."

Wills experienced another serious setback when he learned that Boston's desire for its own cemetery plot caused them to enter into negotiations with McConaughy. The latter probably received his own moment of exasperation when he read of Curtin's and eight other states' agreement to establish a national cemetery at the "point of the desperate attack made upon the left centre of our army" published in the *Adams Sentinel* on August 4. This would be Cemetery Ridge, not adjacent to Evergreen Cemetery on Cemetery Hill. Believing he could never get McConaughy to relinquish his land on Cemetery Hill, Wills began considering land on the adjacent Cemetery Ridge—the site of the Pickett-Pettigrew-Trimble Charge on July 3.

Wills's change of heart may have caused McConaughy to quickly pen an offer of the Cemetery Hill properties to Curtin on August 5, 1863, offering nine acres of the desired land at his own purchase price: $200 an acre. If the Union dead were not to be buried in Evergreen Cemetery, they would at least be buried near it. He offered the land with one caveat: A fence could not be erected between the

David Buehler was an influential member of the Republican Party in 1863. Because he was serving as Gettysburg's postmaster, his wife, Fanny, insisted that he leave the town prior to the appearance of Confederate troops. (achs)

military cemetery and his own Evergreen Cemetery. This stipulation would undoubtedly increase the value of his cemetery plots.

Governor Curtin had his hands full dealing with the myriad of problems that demanded his attention, so the last thing he wanted to do was mediate the dispute between Wills and McConaughy. When the latter expressed his willingness to sell the desired nine acres on Cemetery Hill, Curtin passed the idea onto Wills. "The land referred to is not the same I have been negotiating for—would not be an objectionable location if it could be obtained without certain restrictions," Wills wrote to Curtin on August 7. He also informed Curtin that "[I] have the cooperation personally and by telegraph of a number of states."

Wills was probably so concerned that Curtin would accept McConaughy's offer that he hopped on a train that very night for a meeting he requested with the governor the following day. He successfully lobbied the governor to purchase ten acres on Cemetery Ridge for the new national cemetery. Wills immediately returned to Gettysburg on August 8 and began negotiating with landowners on Cemetery Ridge, for he wrote to Curtin on August 10 of his purchase of "the ten acres of land on the left center with the privilege to take as much more as may be desired" at a price of $200 per acre. Wills followed up the following day with another telegram: "Enclosed please find contract for land I have purchased for the Commonwealth of Pennsylvania." He tried to convince the governor of the support from other states: "There have been several agents here from other states, & all are very much pleased with the location. It is beautiful ground for burial & ornamentation but not quite so elevated as the ground I first wrote you about, but which I failed in buying." He also informed Curtin that his August 1 communication to the seventeen governors had brought twelve into the fold.

Wills's shift to Cemetery Ridge was probably made to maintain the momentum and avoid losing other states' support. It was a far cry from his original letter to Curtin that stated the Cemetery Hill location was most desired "above all others, for the honorable burial of the dead." The way was now clear for Wills to begin planning the new cemetery, or at least so he thought. Dissent about the Cemetery Ridge site was swift and forceful. Thirteen "out-of-towners" and sixteen influential Gettysburg citizens begged Curtin to reconsider the site in a communication dated August 12, 1863.

These were no ordinary citizens, for they included the Presidents of Pennsylvania College and the Lutheran Theological Seminary, influential professors, attorneys, and businessmen. They wrote:

> We are convinced that the site selected by your agent, after he failed in obtaining that adjoining Evergreen Cemetery & forming part of that noble eminence, is by no means a suitable one, and that it would be the subject of lasting regret, if it is employed for that purpose We are happy to learn that the other far more elevated site, commanding a far more extensive view, & being remarkably well adapted for the purpose in view, which your agent failed to select, owing to a misunderstanding concerning the conditions of the offer, is now offered by the Cemetery Board in fee simple, without any restrictions at all.

The communication ended with a plea that Curtin, "send a commission of disinterested gentlemen to the spot, or if possible to visit the place yourself, & decide this matter, so that this grand national enterprise may not be defective in so essential a feature as its location."

Curtin appointed two influential local citizens to mediate the disagreement between McConaughy and Wills. David Buehler was an influential Republican attorney who also served as Gettysburg's postmaster and Edward Fahnestock was a very successful merchant. In recounting their successful conclusion of the negotiations on August 14, 1863, they identified the major roadblock as "the peculiar relations subsisting between them." Cutting through the personal animus, they may have convinced

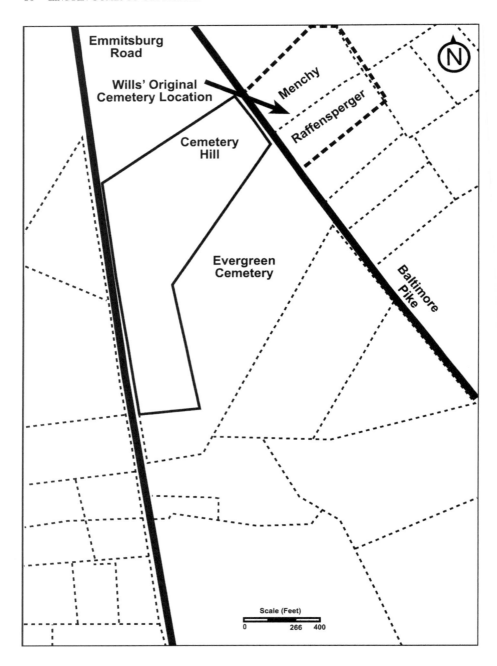

WILLS'S ORIGINAL CONCEPT—David Wills's original concept for the Soldiers' Cemetery encompassed a small area on East Cemetery Hill. Unfortunately for Wills, his adversary, David McConaughy, purchased the acreage before he could secure permission from Governor Curtin to buy it.

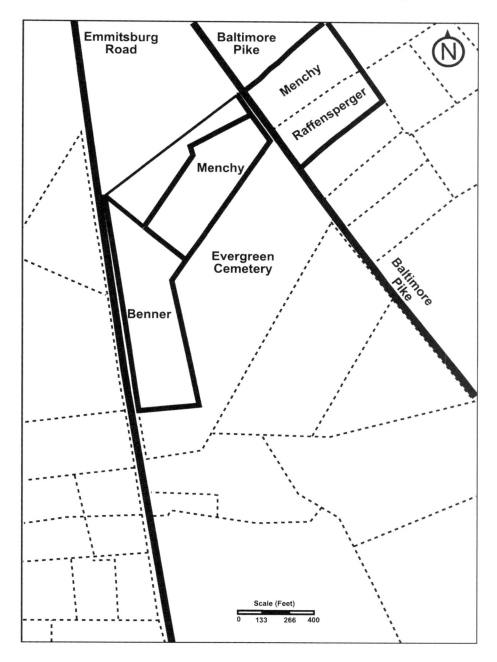

DAVID MCCONAUGHY'S INITIAL PURCHASES—David McConaughy was unsuccessful in integrating the new cemetery into the Evergreen Cemetery, but he did begin the process of purchasing sacred battlefield acreage to keep it from development.

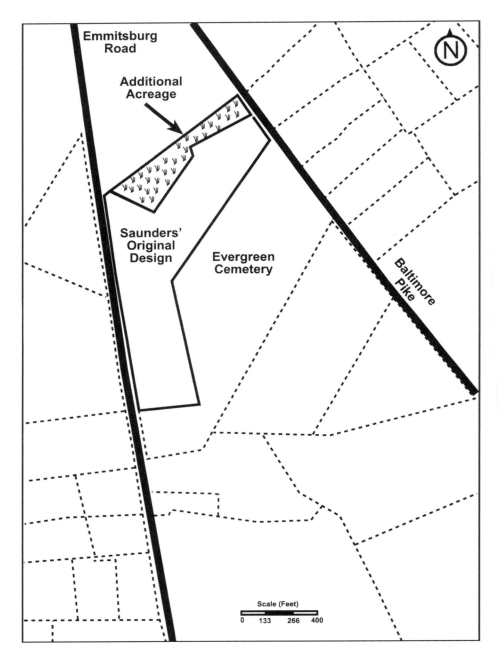

WILLIAM SAUNDERS'S IDEAS—Landscape architect William Saunders liked the site selected for the Soldiers' Cemetery but sought additional acreage along Emmitsburg Road to complete his design.

McConaughy and the rest of the Evergreen Cemetery Board to give on the stipulation of no fence between the two properties. With this understanding, they sat down with Wills and encouraged him to agree to the arrangement. "Mr. Wills finally agreed to accept the more eligible site adjoining the cemetery, if we could guarantee a full and unconditional title to the state."

When approached by Buehler and Fahnestock, the Evergreen Cemetery Board of Directors moved quickly to grease the wheels. They passed a resolution on August 14, 1863 selling the properties McConaughy secured "at the original cost prices" and modified the original stipulation of no fence between

Now part of the Gettysburg National Battlefield on East Cemetery Hill, David Wills initially wanted the land owned by Peter Raffensperger and Mr. Edward Menchy to form the core of the new Soldier's Cemetery. (lg)

the two entities to "an open iron railing enclosure of ordinary height be made and maintained by the State. . . ." McConaughy bolted from the meeting to his office to pen a letter to Gov. Curtin. He wrote, "You seem to have mistaken me. I bought the land for Ever Green Cemetery & with a hope that a satisfactory mutual arrangement could be made for the burial of our soldier dead." He enclosed the Board's resolution and fired both off to Curtin. In their letter to Curtin on August 14, 1863, Buehler and Fahnestock congratulated the governor "upon the satisfactory determination of the matter."

The fight for the location of the new national cemetery was now over, but the hard work of implementing the dream was just beginning. This would involve the tenacity and creativity of David Wills. David McConaughy did not sit back, however. He went right back to work saving valuable battlefield land.

Planning the New National Cemetery

CHAPTER FOUR

August 12-November 17, 1863

David Wills was not about to wait around for the national cemetery's location to be finalized. It was not "if" it would be approved, as much as "where" it would reside. Wills's most important task involved convincing all seventeen governors to participate in the project. He sent each a circular outlining the eight general concepts for the national cemetery on August 12, 1863:

1. *The state of Pennsylvania to purchase the ground, about twelve acres, on the battle field, near the present Gettysburg cemetery, and take the title in fee, and the ground to be devoted in perpetuity to the object.* Wills was careful not to delineate the actual location of the cemetery as it was still being debated. Curtin and Wills apparently believed that the state of Pennsylvania's purchase of the land would remove the roadblock of each governor buying land outside of his own state.

2. *All the bodies of the Soldiers who fell in defence of the Union, to be taken up from the battle field, without necessary delay, and deposited in the cemetery, those that can be designated by name, to be marked by a small head stone, with a number upon it, and the others in a common grave to be marked by some appropriate stone. A record to be kept of the names indicated by the numbers on the stones. The dead of each State, where known, to be buried by themselves, in the particular lot set apart to the state. The whole expense of this, to be carried to a common account.* This was a major departure from Wills's original idea, where the dead

The Soldiers' National Cemetery was intended to be a place for solitude and reflection. This sign seeks to ensure that all continue to respect that tradition of sanctity. (lg)

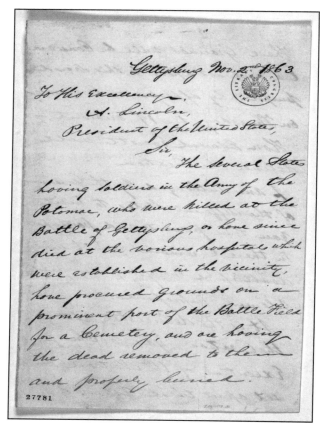

The four-page letter inviting Lincoln to speak at the cemetery's consecration reflected the discord among the planning committee over whether to invite the president to say "a few appropriate remarks." This is the first page of the letter. (loc)

would be buried by "order of companies, regiments, division and Corps, 'without state partitions.'" This would make the cemetery truly a "national soldiers' cemetery, and not a vision of state provincialism," according to Historian Kathy Georg. This change was a nod to states, such as Massachusetts, which forcefully argued for keeping its dead separate from those of other states.

3. *The ground to be enclosed by a well built stone wall, from stone found on or near the premises. Also, a keeper's house to be erected on the lot, at a cost of about $2,000. And the grounds to be tastefully laid out, and adorned with trees & shrubbery, all this expense to be carried to a common account.* This would be changed to a metal fence as part of the agreement with the Evergreen Board of Directors.

4. *A suitable monument to be erected on the ground at the common expense, at a cost not exceeding $10,000, or if it shall cost more, only that sum shall be charged to the common expense.*" Wills apparently "borrowed" this idea from McConaughy.

5. *All the foregoing expenses, stated, to be chargeable to a common account (to wit under heads 2, 3, & 4) are to be apportioned among the several states having soldiers to be buried in the cemetery . . . each state to be assessed according to its population, as indicated by the number of its representatives in Congress.* Wills and Curtin could have accomplished this on the basis of the number of corpses on the field or the number of

regiments hailing from each state, but the easiest and quickest approach was on the basis of number of Congressional representatives from each state. This set up some inequities. For example, the State of Illinois paid $12,000 for its share, but buried only six men. Massachusetts on the other hand, interred 158 men but only paid $8,000. None of the states complained about the approach, though.

6. *After the original outlay the ground to be kept in order, and the house, & fences in repair by the state of Penna.*

7. *It is expressly stipulated that the whole expense, chargeable to the common account, shall not exceed $35,000.*

8. *Each state, if it pleases appoint an agent, who shall act with David Wills, agent for Pennsylvania, and other state agents, in carrying out the foregoing plan.*

Wills ended his correspondence with the governors with a sense of urgency: "It is desirable to have as little delay as possible in getting your reply, as the bodies of our soldiers are, in many cases, so much exposed as to require prompt attention, and the ground should be speedily arranged for their reception."

By August 17, 1863, Wills could report to Curtin that fifteen of the seventeen governors "have already responded, in most instances, pledging their States to unite in the movement; in a few instances, highly approving of the project, and stipulating to urge upon their Legislatures to make appropriations to defray their proportionate share of expense." He also informed Curtin that seventeen acres were now secured for the project and he was working in tandem with the various state agents on the project. The seventeen acres cost $2,475.87. Wills ended his report by suggesting the burials not commence until November out of "proper respect for the health of the community." Opening the graves created significant risks to the civilians and several had already fallen sick. On a more positive note, Wills believed that "the grounds should be artistically laid out, and consecrated by appropriate ceremonies."

Gov. Curtin responded favorably two weeks later: "I am much pleased with the details for the cemetery which you have so thoughtfully

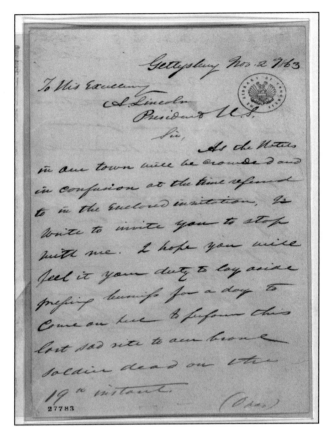

David Wills enclosed a separate letter inviting Lincoln to stay at his home during his visit to Gettysburg. This is the first page of the short letter. (loc)

suggested, and will be glad, so far as is in my power, to hasten their consummation on the part of Pennsylvania." Perhaps worried about the fragile union with the other governors, Curtin warned Wills that some of them "may desire to make some alterations and modifications of your proposed plan of purchasing and managing these sacred grounds, and it is my wish that you give to their views the most careful and respectful consideration." He admitted that "Pennsylvania will be so highly honored by the possession within her limits of this Soldiers' mausoleum . . . that it becomes her duty, as it is her melancholy pleasure, to yield, in every reasonable way, to the wishes, and suggestions, of the States who join with her in dedicating a portion of her territory to the solemn uses of a National sepulcher." Curtin's instructions to Wills were crystal clear—don't do anything to destroy the promise of a national cemetery on Pennsylvania soil.

Wills had apparently not given up on the idea of burying the dead, not by state, but by regiment or where they fell on the battlefield. The August 12 circular clearly informed each governor of the decision to bury the dead by state, but the decision continued gnawing at him, so he fired off another communication to the governors on September 15. "It seems to be the general wish that the stipulation of our Circular of details in reference to the Solders

Cemetery here be so modified that all should be buried together and not separated into States." After providing his rationale, Wills asked, "Will it be agreeable to you to have this modification made?" Many governors responded immediately. Wisconsin governor Edward Salomon's aide responded "the Gov prefers that the Wis. Dead in the battlefield of Gettysburg should be buried together so bringing immediate [illegible] to life together in death." These types of reactions concerned Gov. Curtin. Massachusetts had made it clear that it would bolt the project if its dead were not buried together and now other governors were expressing their displeasure. At the urging of Gov. Curtin, Wills finally threw up his hands and agreed to a segregation of the dead by state.

Scottish-born William Saunders was a botanist and landscape designer working for the U. S. Department of Agriculture at the time of the battle of Gettysburg. He was tapped to design the new cemetery and used his keen eye for design, sight-lines, and love of trees in his planning. (loc)

Wills's "to-do" checklist was getting shorter. He had lined up support for the new national cemetery and purchased the land. Now came the heavy lifting. He still needed to design it, move the bodies to it, and consecrate it. Wills was fortunate to have the services of the country's preeminent landscape architect, William Saunders, who was working for the Superintendent of Horticulture for the U.S. Department of Agriculture at the time. Saunders immigrated to the United States in 1848 and immediately went to work as a landscape designer and horticulturalist. He landscaped large estates and assisted in the layout of New York City's Central Park. Of greatest interest to Wills was probably Saunders's experience in laying out several cemeteries. He was the perfect person to design the new national cemetery.

Wills's invitation to Saunders did not reach him because of mail delays, so it was not until late August that he ventured to Gettysburg. Saunders probably took the train from Washington and then walked the short distance from the Gettysburg train station to the Wills house. After a discussion, the two made their way to Cemetery Hill. Saunders was immediately impressed with the terrain and began mentally laying out the cemetery. He later wrote, "I was pleased with the site, but saw that it was angular, and its front on the Baltimore Pike was only about 150 feet." He told Wills to "get more land!" for the cemetery which would have the effect of "extending the front line and straightening out other lines." Wills immediately went to work and in a short time had possession of an additional five acres of the orchard owned by Capt. John Myers.

Saunders returned to his quarters to ponder his design. The land had definite pluses and minuses. The undulating terrain giving rise to high and low points concerned him for some states "would, of necessity, be placed in the lower portions and thus an apparently unjust discrimination might be inferred." Saunders was savvy enough to understand the politics, so he went to work eliminating this challenge. He decided to avoid this issue by placing the monument on the highest part of the land with the graves in a "semi-circular arrangement [would be] made, so that the appropriation for each State would be a part of a common center and the position of each lot would be relatively of equal importance."

Saunders's design carefully laid out the graves in concentric half circles with the monument in the center. (lg)

With this issue resolved, Saunders went to work laying out the cemetery. "The prevailing expression of the Cemetery should be that of simple grandeur. Simplicity is that element of beauty in a scene that leads gradually from one object to another, in easy

Each section of the cemetery represented a state's dead, and each state marker includes the number of soldiers interred in the section. (lg)

harmony, avoiding abrupt contrasts and unexpected features," he wrote in his report. Saunders was first and foremost a horticulturalist and this certainly showed in his design. "The disposition of trees and shrubs is such as will ultimately produce a considerable degree of landscape effect. Ample spaces of lawn are provided; these will form vistas, as seen from the drive, showing the monument and other prominent points." Saunders understood the disruptive nature of roads and paths, so he kept these to a minimum, noting "roads and walks are exclusively objects of utility; their introduction can only be justified by direct necessity."

Saunders outlined the arrangement of the actual cemetery as follows:

- The ground was marked out in parallels 12 feet in width, thus giving a length of about 7 feet for the interments and 5 feet of pathway between the next parallel.

- On the inner circle of each a heavy line of curbing was placed. This made a continuous circle of gravestones, as it were.

- About 2 1/2 feet was marked on these stones, the width for each interment, and the name carved on the granite at its head.

Each gravestone was to contain the soldier's name, company, and regiment. This grave is President Richard Nixon's great-grandfather, who served in the 73rd Ohio. (lg)

- These blocks showed 10 inches above the surface of the ground and show a width of 10 inches on their upper surface or face.

- The name, company, and regiment being carved in the granite opposite each interment, secured a simple and impressive arrangement, combined with permanence and durability.

Historian Kathy Georg pointed out the striking similarities between McConaughy's original plan and Saunders's ideas, including a central monument surrounded by the soldiers' graves designated by small blocks without regard to rank. She posited that McConaughy likely interacted with Saunders as the two walked their respective pieces of land and the former remained very interested in the design of the fence between the two cemeteries.

When completing his cemetery plans, Saunders needed to know the approximate size of each state's portion. He called upon Wills for this information and he later reported, "this number was obtained by having a thorough search made for all the graves, and a complete list of the names accurately taken."

Saunders's design was quickly embraced by all involved. Later, as the date of consecration ceremony approached, Saunders was called to the White House to meet with President Lincoln to discuss the cemetery's design. The meeting occurred on November 17, 1863, and Saunders recounted the meeting as: "I... spread the plans on his office table," Saunders recalled. "He took much interest in it, asked about its surroundings, about Culp's Hill, Round Top, etc. and seemed familiar with the topography of the place although he had never been there. He was much pleased with the method of the graves, said it differed from the ordinary cemetery, and, after I had explained the reasons, said it was an advisable and benefitting arrangement." Historian Martin Johnson believed Lincoln was not merely interested in the arrangement of the graves, but used the visit and knowledge to help him frame his remarks during the consecration ceremony.

Moving the Corpses

CHAPTER FIVE
October 5, 1863-March 25, 1864

Despite the unusually high number of Gettysburg residents becoming ill during the autumn, David Wills understood the importance of moving the corpses expeditiously to the newly established national cemetery. He later reported his rationale:

> *The marks at the graves were but temporary; in many instances, a small rough board, on which the name was faintly written with a lead pencil. This would necessarily be effaced by the action of the weather, and the boards were also liable to be thrown down and lost. The graves which were unmarked were in many instances level with the surface of the earth, and the grass and weeds were growing over them; and in the forests, the fall of the leaves in the autumn would cover them so that they might be entirely lost.*

He obviously could not begin the process until successfully securing the land and ensuring acceptance of Saunders's layout of the cemetery. He was ready by October 15, 1863, when he placed a request for proposals in local newspapers for moving the corpses to the new cemetery.

Wills carefully laid out the requirements for the bidders. There were two pieces to the process: removing the bodies from their shallow graves on

Two entrances grace the Soldiers' National Cemetery. This entrance is off of Taneytown Road and serves as the major entry point for most visitors to the cemetery. (lg)

James Townsend of Rahway, New Jersey, was hired by David Wills to serve as surveyor and superintendent of burials. The position involved carefully observing the re-burial of the corpses in the Soldiers' Cemetery and keeping a running tally, which he shared with David Wills each evening. He was known for his meticulous work. (achs)

the battlefield and interring them in the national cemetery. A contractor could bid on one or both pieces. Wills explained that coffins would first be procured from the train station, but only the number actually to be used on a given day could be removed. After picking up the coffins, the wagons headed to that part of the battlefield where the corpses were being removed. Wills was very specific about how the bodies were to be disinterred: "He shall open up the grave or trench where the dead are buried, and carefully take out the remains and place them in a coffin, and screw down the lid tight, and nail the head-board, where the grave has been marked, carefully on the lid of the coffin. He shall then re-place all blankets, &c., that may have been taken out of the grave and not put around the body, back in the grave, and close it up, neatly leveling it over."

The coffins were then to be loaded back onto the wagons and taken to the cemetery. Wills specified a maximum of 100 coffins could be transported to the cemetery each day. The successful bidder would presumably have a crew at the cemetery preparing the graves to receive the coffins. Wills expected the grave sites to be "dug in trenches, and the coffins placed in them side by side, of the number in each trench designated by the plot of the grounds." The trench would be three feet deep and as wide as the coffin. He also expected a twenty-inch hole dug at the head of each grave that was two feet deep and lined with stones. "The coffins shall then be placed in the grave, side by side, as ordered by the superintendent—the head-board of each one nailed upright against the head of the coffin, and of sufficient height above the ground not to conceal the lettering when the grave is filled up. The grave must then be filled up a sufficient height, in the opinion of the superintendent, to prevent settling below the surface."

The successful contractor could expect payment on "Saturday evening of every week for the full amount of the work done." Finally, a bond would be required in the amount of $3,000 "for the faithful performance of the contract, with two or more sureties, to be approved by David Wills." The work was to commence on October 26, 1863—less than a week after the bids were opened on October 22, 1863.

Wills eagerly reviewed the proposals after the deadline passed and was pleased by the high number of responses—34. The quotes ranged from $1.59 to $8.00 per corpse for the entire job. He probably knew Frank W. Biesecker and quickly accepted his low bid of $1.59 per body. Wills made two other important hires: James S. Townsend of Rahway, New Jersey, and Samuel Weaver, a local man who opened Gettysburg's first photographic

studio in 1852 and ran it until 1860, when at the age of 48, he turned it over to his son, Peter. Weaver would oversee the process of disinterring the bodies as Superintendent of Exhuming the Bodies; Townsend as Surveyor and Superintendent of Burials would watch over their interments.

David Wills received 34 bids in response to his request for proposals to move the corpses to the new cemetery. He was very pleased by the response and paid less per body than he predicted. (gnmp).

The contractor's responsibilities of disinterring bodies from the battlefield and re-interring them in the national cemetery was too big a job, so Frank Biesecker subcontracted with Basil Biggs who in turn hired 10-12 free African Americans to disinter the corpses. Biggs stood by as his men unsealed every grave. He would gain fame for his careful and diligent work on this project. Biggs had at least two teams transporting the coffins. First thing in the morning, David Warren and his fifteen-year-old son, Leander, drove their wagon to the train station to pick up six coffins and deliver them to the battlefield. After unloading them, the father and son returned to the station for another

Diminutive and bearded Samuel Weaver was a well-known figure in Gettysburg, having opened its first photographic studio in 1852. David Wills tapped Weaver to be the superintendent of exhuming the bodies. Working with Basil Biggs and his crew, Weaver oversaw the opening of each grave, determined whether it was a Union or Confederate soldier, attempted to identify it, and then watched as it was carefully placed in a wooden coffin. (gnmp)

wagon-load. Upon unloading this supply of empty coffins, the original six coffins, each now filled with a corpse, were loaded onto the wagon for the trip to the national cemetery. With the unloading of the wagon, the Warrens headed back to the train station for another load of coffins. Biggs had another wagon team, this one with a nine-coffin capacity, that also rode the circuit.

Weaver closely watched the workers uncover each gravesite and carefully remove the corpse. He now went to work attempting to identify the dead soldier. Weaver surely appreciated legible headboards, but where not present or illegible, he had the onerous chore of going through the dead soldier's pockets for "letters, papers, receipts, certificates, diaries, memorandum books, photographs, marks on the clothing, belts, or cartridge boxes, &c." to find hints of his identity. Rifling through a deteriorating corpses' clothing and personal effects is a gruesome task and Weaver made it a bit easier by employing an iron hook to reach into pockets. Because Wills understood and appreciated Weaver's thankless task, his report heaped lavish praise on him, noting the success of the process was "owing in part to the great care and attention bestowed by Mr. Samuel Weaver, whom I employed to superintend the exhuming of the bodies. Through his untiring and faithful efforts, the bodies in many unmarked graves have been identified in various ways."

As the corpse was lowered into the coffin, Weaver wrote the soldier's name, company, and regiment on the coffin's lid and issued it a number, which he carefully recorded in his log book. Weaver brought this book to David Wills each evening. Wagons now brought the bodies to the cemetery where James Townsend was waiting for them. As the "Surveyor and Superintendent of Burials," Townsend supervised trench digging to ensure compliance with Wills's specifications. It appears Frank Biesecker and John Hoke dug at least some of the graves. At the end of each day, Townsend brought the daily total to Wills's office, where it was compared with Weavers' tally.

The process of disinterring the dead, transporting them to the cemetery, and reburying them was a time-consuming process. The first dead were processed on October 27, 1863, and the work halted twice: during the consecration ceremony on November 19, 1863, and later when the frozen ground made digging impossible. The February 15, 1864, edition of the *Gettysburg Compiler* reported "the bodies of about 3,100 Federal soldiers have been reburied in the National Cemetery. Several hundred are yet to be removed." The last body was buried on March 18, 1864. Samuel Weaver noted the "number of bodies exceeding our first calculations," which extended the length of the process. James Townsend added, "[O]ccasionally, the wet weather and the snows would stop the work, so that it has been protracted much beyond the time we at first anticipated having it completed. Wills's paid employees ultimately buried 3,354 bodies in the national cemetery. Preferring to oversee the removal of their own dead, Boston hired local stone-cutter Solomon Powers to process its 158 corpses, so the total number of Union dead buried in the cemetery numbered 3,512.

Because the Union dead were promiscuously buried throughout the battlefield, Wills worried about missing some of them. He enlisted the help of local farmers in identifying burial sites by placing advertisements in the local newspapers. He wrote, "many [graves] have been buried in secluded spots and persons [farmers] will confer a great favor by making known to me or to Mr. Samuel Weaver . . ."

Not all of the dead were in the same condition, as Weaver's crews quickly learned, and this had a direct bearing on the ability to ascertain the identity of the corpse. Weaver noted in his report that those dead on the July 1 battleground lie in the open air from at least July 1 through July 5 because it was occupied by the enemy. Some of these bodies were not buried for a number of days even after the area was reclaimed by Union troops and were often

Samuel Weaver gave his photographic studio to his son, Peter, prior to the outbreak of the Civil War. Weaver's photos of Camp Letterman are vital in understanding this large hospital northeast of town. The same is true of Weaver's photographs of the cemetery's consecration. (achs)

"covered with a small portion of earth dug up from along side of the body. This left them much exposed to the heat, air, and rains, and they decomposed rapidly, so that when these bodies were taken up, there was nothing remaining but the dry skeleton." Weaver noted that "the consequence was, that but few on the battle field of July 1st, were marked."

Weaver and his men appreciated bodies buried in a clay substrate or marshy areas for they were fairly well preserved, and it was easier to ascertain the soldier's identity. Those buried in sandy, porous soil were "entirely decomposed." Despite these setbacks, Weaver was able to identify a majority of the bodies. He admitted that 975 bodies had no sign of name, unit, or even state designation and in other cases Weaver could identify the state the corpses hailed from, but nothing else, so they were buried in that appropriate state's plot.

Careful analyses reveal a number of instances where a body was misidentified, usually because it contained items from another soldier. For example, one body had an inscribed medal with the name Private Levi Bulla and that name is on the grave. However, the real Private Bulla survived the war and died in Kansas in the 1880s. Several soldiers, for some reason, carried the letters of others or equipment stenciled with the name of another, and this led to their graves being incorrectly marked. At least three soldiers listed as being buried in the cemetery actually died before the battle, another three survived but died before the end of the war, and fourteen survived the war. A number of soldiers were buried in the correct grave, but their name was misspelled, leading to confusion. For example, William E. Barrows of the 19th Maine Infantry is identified as E. E. Burrows on the headstone. John Busey estimates fully a quarter of all gravestones have errors in spelling or unit numbers/designations.

Weaver took his job very seriously. He reported,

There was not a grave permitted to be opened or a body searched unless I was present. I was inflexible in enforcing this rule, and here can say, with the greatest satisfaction to myself and to the friends of the soldiers, that I saw everybody taken out of its temporary resting place, and all the pockets carefully searched; and where the grave was not marked, I examined all the clothing and everything about the body to find the name. I then saw the body, with all the hair and all the particles of bone, carefully placed in the coffin, and if there was a head-board, I required it to be at once nailed to the coffin. - At the same time, I wrote the name, company, and regiment, of the soldier on the coffin, and numbered the coffin, and entered in my book the same endorsement.

Farmer, teamster, and veterinarian Basil Biggs (foreground) was one of the leaders in Gettysburg's African American community. He moved his family to Gettysburg from Maryland in the 1850s so his children could receive an education. He was hired by Samuel Weaver to directly oversee the crews unearthing the corpses. His earnings made him one of the wealthiest African Americans in Gettysburg, and he used them to purchase a farm outside of town. (achs)

This remarkable shot shows Samuel Weaver, with notebook in hand to the right, overseeing the removal of a corpse from the battlefield. He used a metal hook to remove the contents of the men's pockets and wrote each soldier's name and unit on the lid of the casket. (gnmp)

This onerous task was made more difficult, Weaver complained, by individuals who got to the grave before his crew and "obliterating and destroying many originally well preserved graves, by opening them carelessly and leaving about the area open graves, bones, clothing, and hair."

Weaver carefully bundled items of value when found, including letters, money, and diaries. These 287 packets were given to David Wills for distribution to the dead soldiers' family. The number actually finding their way to loved ones is not known. A whopping $36 in gold was found in the pockets of one corpse and $30-40 in others. There was simply no time to try to seek out the relatives, Wills explained, so the packets were "properly labeled, and held in safekeeping for the relatives, should they ever call for them."

All involved in this sacred undertaking worried that some Confederates might accidentally make their way into the cemetery reserved for the Union dead. Weaver attempted to allay fears by addressing the issue at the conclusion of his report. He asserted he could easily identify a Rebel corpse:

> *In the first place, as a general rule, the rebels never went into battle with the United States coat on. They sometimes stole the pantaloons from our dead and wore them, but not the coat. The rebel clothing is made of cotton, and is of a grey or brown color.*

Occasionally I found one with a blue cotton jean roundabout on. The clothing of our men is of wool, and blue; so that the body having the coat of our uniform on was a pretty sure indicator that he was a Union soldier. But if the body were without a coat, then there were other infallible marks. The shoes of the rebels were differently made from those of our soldiers. If these failed, then the underclothing was the next part examined. The rebel cotton undershirt gave proof of the army to which he belonged. In no instance was a body allowed to be removed which had any portion of the rebel clothing on it. Taking all these things together, we never had much trouble in deciding, with infallible accuracy, whether the body was that of a Union soldier or a rebel.

Fourteen-year-old Leander Warren (this photo shows him later in life) assisted his father in picking up coffins from the train station every day, delivering them to the part of the battlefield where the corpses were being disinterred, and then carrying the filled coffins to the new Soldiers' Cemetery. He would later travel south with Joseph Townsend, who was surveying confiscated land in South Carolina. An outbreak of yellow fever sent him home, but only after Townsend had succumbed to the disease. (achs)

Weaver did err occasionally for we know of as many as eight Confederates buried in the national cemetery.

Wills was delighted with the quality of the work. He noted in his final report that the work of Biesecker was performed with "great care and to my entire satisfaction." The project's total cost of $80,000 exceeded his earlier prediction. On March 25, 1864, the Commonwealth of Pennsylvania officially incorporated the ground as the "Soldiers' National Cemetery. It was later transferred to the U. S. Department of War on May 1, 1872, and is now one of 130 national cemeteries that enshrine our fallen heroes.

But what of the Confederate dead? A story in the March 22, 1864, edition of the *Adams County Sentinel* estimated "not less than seven thousand Rebels lost their lives in this conflict." The Sentinel worried that the shallow enemy graves would be "obliterated" when the farmers began plowing their fields in the spring in preparation for a new growing season. "There is a strong desire with the people, in respect to humanity, to have these bodies, though of the enemy, respectfully and decently put away, in some enclosure where they may not be disturbed— where they can sleep in quietude." This would not occur until 1871.

Planning the Consecration Ceremony

CHAPTER SIX

August 17-November 18, 1863

David Wills pushed for a consecration ceremony as early as August 17, 1863, in a letter to Pennsylvania Gov. Curtin. The governor replied two weeks later: "The proper consecration of the grounds must claim our early attention; and, as soon as we can do so, our fellow-purchasers should be invited to join with us in the performance of suitable ceremonies on the occasion." This added yet another obligation to Wills's responsibilities. It is a wonder he spent any time with his pregnant wife and children during this period.

Keeping with the custom of the times, Wills knew he needed to build the ceremony around a gifted orator. This was not a difficult decision as Edward Everett was just the man. Sixty-nine-year old Everett was an ordained minister, a former Harvard faculty member and president, four-term governor of Massachusetts, five-term Congressman in the U.S. House of Representatives, Secretary of State, Ambassador to Britain, and U.S. Senator. Perhaps most of all, Everett was considered the preeminent orator of the period. Governor Curtin concurred with Wills's suggestion and so did the governors and state agents. Wills wrote to Everett on September 23, 1863, explaining the concept of the Soldiers' National Cemetery and the desire to consecrate it on October 23, 1863, "with appropriate

Most experts now believe the speakers' platform was actually in the Evergreen Cemetery, close to the gravesite of Jennie Wade. Her grave can be seen in the background, marked by a statue and American flag. (lg)

Edward Everett was the greatest orator of his time and, combined with his impeccable credentials, he was a natural to give the major address at the cemetery's consecration ceremony. (loc)

ceremonies." He informed Everett that "the several States interested, have united in the selection of you to deliver the oration on that solemn occasion. I am therefore instructed, by the Governors of the different States interested in this project, to invite you cordially to join with them in the ceremonies, and to deliver the oration for the occasion."

Everett was a much sought after speaker and the short notice made it likely he would reject the invitation. Everett responded on October 26: "I feel much complimented by this request, and would cheerfully undertake the performance of a duty at once so interesting and honorable." However, Everett noted the ceremony's proposed date was out of the question. "I am under engagements which will occupy all my time from Monday next to the 12th of October, and, indeed, it is doubtful whether, during the whole month of October, I shall have a day at my command." He proposed moving the consecration to a later date when his schedule was freer and he had more time to prepare for an "occasion . . . of great importance."

In an era without television, radio, or movies, formal orations served as a popular form of entertainment and information. It became something of an art form, and it was not unusual for such a speech to last one or even two hours. Everett made it clear he intended to give full attention to his remarks, spending time learning about the battle, walking the battlefield, determining how it fit with the larger context of the war before carefully crafting his remarks. Speakers of the day memorized their long speeches and Everett intended to do just that.

Wills carefully weighed his options. He could move the ceremony to November 19, but risk less temperate weather that could wreak havoc on the ceremony. Yet, if moving the event a month later meant netting the most distinguished speaker in the United States, then so be it. The date was set and the rest of the planning commenced.

Similar to a current-day rockstar, Everett made other demands on Wills. Because of failing health, the 69-year-old requested a tent next to the speakers' platform where he could rest and reflect in relative quiet. Kidney problems also required a place where Everett could make a quick exit to empty his bladder. He also wished the cemetery burials would begin prior to the ceremony to lend more meaning to his words. This request was not a problem. Wills's request for proposals to move the dead was due on October 22 and the first burials were to begin on October 26. The original timeline would have put the consecration ceremony a few days before the burials commenced, but the date change allowed the process to be well underway by the time Everett took center stage.

Wills went to work finalizing the remainder of the program. Scrutinizing other consecration ceremonies, Wills understood the need for music and prayers. The *Adams Sentinel* noted: "Music is the most delightful rational entertainment that the human mind can possibly enjoy." However, for this sacred event, music was much more than that—"it was the revelation of the soul of a people who knew the exaltation of victory, the bitterness of defeat, and the sorrow of irreparable loss," according to Professor Kenneth A. Bernard. Wills invited four bands to participate in the ceremony—others would come on their own. Those asked included: the United States Marine Band, Birgfeld's Band of Philadelphia, the Second United States Artillery Band of Philadelphia, and the Band of the Fifth New York Artillery. All would march in the procession to the platform, but only the first two would sound notes during the actual ceremony. Adolph Birgfield's band was sometimes referred to as Birgfield's German Band because of the preponderance of immigrants. It was a renowned group under a talented leader who would compose a piece for the consecration ceremony. Francis Scala's Marine Band would perform the second number. A favorite of the president, its selection was an easy one.

Adolf Birgfield led the Birgfield Band of Philadelphia. It earned a special place on the program because it was a favorite of Gov. Andrew Curtin. The band accompanied Curtin on the train to Gettysburg. When the train broke down, the band played to cheer the disgruntled passengers. (fag)

Twenty-year-old Francis Scala emigrated from Italy and immediately joined the U. S. Navy, becoming a member of the Marine Band. His musical talents were noted, and he rose in the ranks, finally becoming the leader of the band in 1855. He regularly performed at the White House and knew all of the presidents until he retired in 1871. (wc)

The Marine Band was formed by an Act of Congress in 1798 and is America's oldest continuously active professional musical organization. This photograph was taken in 1864. (loc)

An invocation was sandwiched between opening musical numbers and Rev. T. H. Stockton was tapped to provide it. As the highly respected Chaplain of the House of Representatives, Stockton was another easy choice. The selection of Rev. Henry L. Baugher, President of Pennsylvania College, to give the closing benediction was a nod to Gettysburg civilians who had suffered so much during the battle and its aftermath.

Wills believed a "dirge" or "ode" would be appropriate for the ceremony and he approached eminent poet, Henry Wadsworth Longfellow, on October 5 to "prepare for us suitable words and I will have them set to music by one of the best composers in the Country." Longfellow begged off so Wills next approached William Cullen Bryant to do the honors. Bryant also rejected the invitation, citing two reasons: "pressure of other occupations and the want of leisure; the other is the difficulty which I experience, of satisfying myself in the composition of poems for public occasions, and which has forced me, for many years past, to leave these tasks to younger men." A determined David Wills next approached John Greenleaf Whittier and then Georg Boker. Each rejected Wills's entreaties. When Benjamin French, a close associate of Lincoln (see below) heard Wills speak of his frustration in finding a suitable poet to compose the ode, he immediately volunteered to compose one. It would ultimately be sung by National Union Musical Association of Maryland. One additional musical

number, a dirge penned by James G. Percival and set to music by Alfred Delaney, was also included in the program. The dirge was dedicated to Gov. Andrew Curtin and would be sung by local choir members, accompanied by Birgfield's band.

Wills was wise enough to realize the demands on him as state agent augmented by overseeing the burial process at the new cemetery prevented him from devoting his full attention to the myriad of tasks associated with planning a smooth consecration ceremony. He therefore approached Lincoln's associate, Ward Lamon, to serve as "Marshal-in-Chief" to oversee the planning and implementation of the consecration ceremony. Gov. Curtin possibly suggested Lamon to Wills. Curtin had strong relationships with Judge Joseph Casey, a former Pennsylvania Congressman, and John Forney, owner of the *Philadelphia Press* and *Washington Chronicle*. Both knew Lamon quite well and were undoubtedly quick to suggest him to Curtin. The decision to tap Lamon was "a stroke of genius," according to historian Frank Klement. Alongside his wide circle of acquaintants, which elevated the stature of the ceremony, Lamon had two other attributes making him an attractive choice: He possessed excellent attention to detail—a vital attribute to organizing this complex event. And his strong personal relationship with Lincoln made the president's presence at the ceremony more probable.

Lamon met Lincoln in 1847 and became a close friend. They could not have been more different. According to Frank Klement, "Lamon was stout, most handsome, and possessed of a swashbuckling air; Lincoln was tall, lean, nearly ugly, and modest in a strange way." Lincoln was an introvert; Lamon an extrovert. One was a heavy drinker, the other preached temperance, yet their love of story and many hours riding together as young lawyers on the judicial circuit bound them together. When Lincoln ascended to the presidency, Lamon became his bodyguard, troubleshooter, and more formally, U.S. Marshal for the District

Henry Baugher was president of Pennsylvania College at the time of the battle and consecration ceremony. He was a Lutheran minister before coming to the college as a faculty member of Greek and belles lettres. He rose to the college's presidency in 1850 and remained in this position until his death in 1868. (achs)

Rev. T. H. Stockton was another easy choice for the consecration program, as he served as the chaplain of the U. S. House of Representatives for many years. He also served as the pastor of the First Methodist Church in Philadelphia and was the editor of *Christian World.* (fommc)

of Columbia. One could observe Lamon standing close by Lincoln at public functions, keeping an eye on all who approached the president.

Wills's invitation to Lamon was penned in a letter dated October 30, 1863: "We have agreed upon you as the proper person, and therefore extend to you an invitation to act as Marshal," he wrote. Wills hoped Lamon would "feel it his duty" to accept, but Lamon was ambivalent, having planned to bring his wife from Illinois to Washington in mid-November. A vacillating Lamon asked Lincoln's counsel. The president wrote to Lamon's father-in-law and his former law-partner a few days later: "He came to me and I told him I thought that in view of his relation to the government and to me, he could not well decline."

The list of Lamon's tasks was long and varied and he dug in with vim and vigor. One of Lamon's first acts was appointing Benjamin French to be his assistant. A historian called it "good sense." French had met Lincoln the same year as Lamon—1847— when he was serving as the Clerk for the U.S. House of Representatives and Lincoln was a newly minted Congressman from Illinois. When French sought re-election to his post, Lincoln voted against him. French later became the head of the Republican Association of Washington in 1857 and played an important role in helping secure Lincoln's election win. He was named Marshal-in-Chief for the inauguration ceremonies and, as a result, had numerous interactions with Lincoln and his associates. Lincoln later nominated him to the post of Commissioner of Public Buildings in the District of Columbia. One of French's responsibilities was standing between Mr. and Mrs. Lincoln at the receiving line, where he introduced guests to the First Family. He developed a deep respect for the president and a rare positive working relationship with the First Lady. French and Lamon became fast friends because they spent so much time together. Having someone as experienced in planning complex ceremonies made good sense to Lamon, so he invited French to be his assistant.

The two men immediately went to work ascertaining the order of the procession. Military units under the supervision of Department of the Susquehanna District Commander, Maj. Gen. Darius Couch, would lead the procession. They would be followed by the chief marshal, the president, the cabinet, the general-in-chief of the army, the judges of the Supreme Court, Edward Everett, the governors, state representatives with their flags flying behind them, the vice president and speaker of the House of Representatives, members of Congress, mayors of cities, members of the organizing committee, and representatives of a myriad of other organizations, such as telegraph companies, hospital corps, and relief organizations. Thousands of civilians would also march in the procession. It would be a long and colorful column making its way to the cemetery.

With the order of the procession established, Lamon went to work determining how such a long column—as many as 10,000 to 15,000 folks— should be organized. He decided to shorten the initial column by using three of the four streets radiating from the town square. The head of the column would form on Carlisle Street, north of the Square, civic bodies would come together on York Street on the east of the Square. The rear of the column, composed mainly of civilians, organized by state, would form on Chambersburg Street to the west of the Square. Marshals were to spread out to ensure order. At "precisely ten o'clock, A.M." the head of the column was to move around the Square and enter Baltimore Street, and move south toward the cemetery.

The column would turn right onto Emmitsburg Road (now Steinwehr) south of town and make a left onto Taneytown Road. Members of the column would easily feel the rise in the road signifying they were scaling Cemetery Hill. As the head of column approached the cemetery, the military units would peel off and line the road to salute the president as he rode past. After the procession passed they would occupy the space to the left of the speakers'

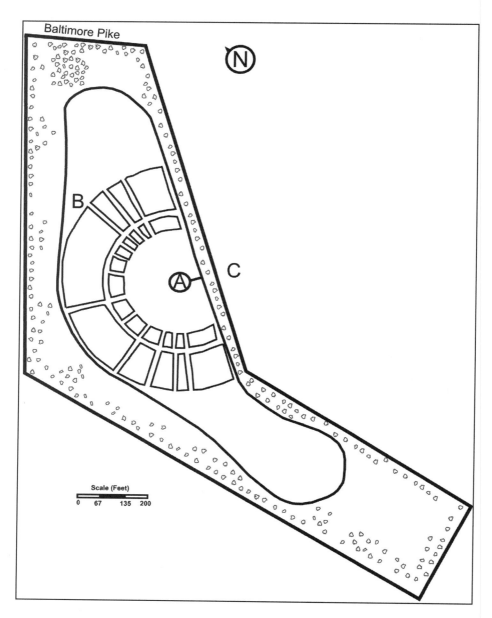

THE SPEAKERS' PLATFORM—The location of the speakers' platform has been debated. Period newspapers and recollections placed it in the current monument's location (A). W. Yates Selleck, Wisconsin's agent, believed it was outside of the graves (B). National Park Service historian Kathleen Georg Harrison used photographic evidence to place it within the confines of the Evergreen Cemetery (C). (lg)

platform. Civilians would occupy the front of the platform; the "ladies" to the right of it.

Lamon and French mulled over other smaller details. The parade marshals would be put on horses, not ride in carriages, and would don distinctive attire: a plain black suit (preferably a frock coat), black hat, white gloves, fringed white satin scarf (five inches wide) worn over the right shoulder, snaking across the breast to the left hip attached in place by a four-inch wide rosette, raised in the middle made of black and white ribbon. Another rosette of red, white, and blue (with the state in the center) was to adorn the left breast. Finally, the saddle cloths were to be of white cambric bordered with black. Lamon called a meeting of the marshals at the courthouse the night before the ceremony and at its conclusion.

Ward Lamon, an attorney and close friend of Abraham Lincoln, played a major role in designing the consecration ceremony. Even a cursory review of the documents suggests the meticulousness of his planning. (loc)

Protecting the president was always on Lamon's mind. He worried about how to maintain order with thousands crowding into the small town. He decided to invite every U.S. Marshal in the eastern half of the United States to act as his assistants during the ceremony. He also invited all the governors whose states had lost sons at Gettysburg to attend the consecration ceremony. Lamon was disappointed by the poor responses—and, in some cases, no responses—to his invitations. Many had a good excuse for missing the ceremony as they received invitations either just before the ceremony or even after it concluded. Lamon was also instrumental in securing additional horses from the army. Between this source and the Commonwealth of Pennsylvania, Lamon collected about 130 horses for the ceremony. No carriages would dot the procession—dignitaries and the marshals would ride on horseback.

Benjamin French assisted Ward Lamon in organizing the consecration event. When the need for an ode arose, French immediately volunteered to create one. (loc)

Lamon received an update from David Wills on November 10—a mere nine days before the ceremony. Wills anticipated an "impressive procession" as many dignitaries were expected to participate and a "tremendous crowd" because the railroads promised to run special trains for the event. Perhaps worried about some items falling

A distinguished former governor and senator representing New York, William Seward battled Lincoln for the Republican nomination to become president. Although an adversary, Lincoln made him secretary of state, and he became one of the president's leading supporters. (loc)

through the cracks, Wills asked Lamon to arrive at Gettysburg a few days early.

Lamon and French complied with Wills's wishes and headed to Gettysburg on November 12. The visit was so important to Wills that when Lamon and French missed their railroad connection for the last leg of the trip from Hanover Junction to Gettysburg, he arranged for a special train to complete the journey. The two men walked the short distance to the Eagle Hotel on Chambersburg Street where they met Wills. They then walked to Wills's office for several hours of conversation. The three discussed plans for the procession and ceremony and Wills explained the details of the program and expressed sincere disappointment when he recounted his frustrations in not being able to secure a proper ode (see above). It was during this conversation that French blurted out that he would pen the important piece and even have it ready by the following day. The result was a piece composed of five, six-line stanzas entitled, "Consecration Hymn."

Details for the ceremony complete, Lamon and French returned to Washington. Lamon realized he needed competent aides during the pre-ceremony set up, and asked several associates to meet with him and French on November 16. Promising free transportation to Gettysburg, Lamon was able to enlist nine additional men. The group decided to leave Washington at 3:00 p.m. the next day. Benjamin French expressed concerns about the late hour and suggested a morning departure. He was overruled and the main party left at the appointed time on November 17. French, still worried about the arduous trip, left at 6:30 a.m., arriving in Gettysburg at 1:30 p.m. As French predicted, Lamon's trains encountered difficulty and did not arrive until the morning of November 18. Wills, Lamon, and French met later that morning to fine tune their arrangements and then walked to the square where they watched as a giant flag was hoisted to the top of a newly erected 60-foot flagpole. They took some time to tour the battlefield and later that evening walked to the train station to greet a very special guest.

Selecting the location of the speakers' platform was an important task addressed by Wills, Lamon, and French as they toured the cemetery on November 13. The 12-foot-by-20-foot platform had to be large enough to host the 30 or more distinguished officials and guests and at the same time be accessible along the parade route and provide good sightlines to and from the audience. It is therefore hard to imagine the location of such an important edifice is the topic of debate. One magazine article called it the "New Battle of Gettysburg." The earliest accounts placed the platform where the Soldiers' National Monument was later erected. Clark Carr, a member of the Soldiers' Cemetery Commission, strongly believed this was the site and he was supported by a host of historians up to 1960. Critics argued such a site would have the 15,000 or so attendees trampling on newly buried graves. Not so fast, said Gettysburg National Military Park historian Frederick Tilberg. There were only 1,250 men buried by November 19 and the numerous assistant marshals would have kept the crowd away from them.

Salmon Chase was a former Ohio governor and candidate for president in the 1860 campaign. Lincoln chose to keep his political enemy close by appointing him secretary of the treasury. He continued to be an adversary until Lincoln appointed him to the Supreme Court in 1864. (loc)

Two documents from Wisconsin agent W. Yates Selleck became available in 1960. Selleck, who claimed to be on the speakers' platform during the ceremony on November 19, noted its location on a map of the cemetery. He placed the location on the northwest edge of the grave sites. From this site, Selleck could see the beleaguered town in front of him, the graves behind him and Seminary Ridge to his left. Selleck recalled hearing the bands play, the recited prayers, Everett's oration, and Lincoln's consecration. Historian R. Gerald McMurtry pinpointed the platform's location as "350 feet almost due north of the Soldiers' National Monument, and forty feet from a point in the outer circle of lots where Michigan and New York sections are separated by a path."

Tilberg challenged Selleck's positioning of the platform, writing, "I studied accounts of

Attorney John Usher, who rode the legal circuit with Abraham Lincoln before the war, was appointed secretary of the interior on January 1, 1863. He was one of three Cabinet secretaries who accompanied Lincoln to Gettysburg. (loc)

the ceremonies in approximately 20 different newspapers" and the location of the platform was clearly in the current location of the national monument. For example, just days after the ceremony, the *Indianapolis Daily Journal* reported, "The platform . . . was erected nearly on the line of the diameter across the semi-circle of the Cemetery, and the crowd filled the interior," and the July 11, 1865, issue of the *Adams Sentinel* noted the platform "was erected in the center of the cemetery, where the monument is to be located," when reporting on the cornerstone-laying ceremony for the new national monument. Tilberg also noted many witnesses "spoke of the high elevation of the spot and the panoramic view. The site advanced by the dissenting side is not on high ground." Four days after the ceremony, the *Pittsburgh Daily Commercial* wrote, "The platform was erected on a beautiful knoll, nearly in the center of the cemetery ground."

One of Tilberg's successors, Kathleen Georg Harrison, threw a third site into the mix. She posited the platform was actually in Evergreen Cemetery, not far from where the National Cemetery's monument would be erected. The speakers would have looked down on the audience, whose backs were to the growing Soldiers' National Cemetery. Strong photographic evidence supports this claim, especially an analysis by William Frassanito, the "dean" of Gettysburg photography, but historian Frank Klement discounted this argument on the basis of the ongoing feud between Wills and McConaughy. Why would McConaughy have permitted his bitter enemy to erect the platform on his cemetery's grounds, he wondered?

Most current historians seem to accept the Evergreen Cemetery location, based mainly on photographic evidence and the Military Park personnel have followed suit. Still to be explained, however, is why virtually every period newspaper clearly placed the platform at the current location of the Soldier's National Cemetery monument.

Wills received assurances from Lamon that the president would most likely attend the ceremony, but Wills decided to formalize the request in a letter to the president on November 2. After explaining the concept of the national cemetery, Wills got right to the point: "We hope you will be able to be present to perform this last solemn act to the soldiers dead on this Battle Field." The timing of the letter and its contents have created a firestorm of controversy almost from the time Wills wrote it. Some historians believe the late date of the invitation to Lincoln suggests it was an afterthought since the date of the ceremony was set at least a month earlier. However, Gov. Curtin may have verbally invited Lincoln to participate in October and Wills may have been following up with his initial invitation on November 2.

Montgomery Blair served as postmaster general in the Lincoln administration and accompanied him to Gettysburg. A West Pointer, he resigned his commission after the Seminole War to become a successful lawyer prior to the outbreak of the war. (loc)

The commissioners did not expect Lincoln to attend the event as the cemetery was not at that time part of the federal government, nor was it anticipated to be. The corporation, governed by representatives of each state whose sons had fought at Gettysburg, did not concentrate on inviting Lincoln. He was informed of the date, as were hundreds of other elected officials, as a courtesy. They were therefore shocked when they learned that Lincoln intended to be present. Why would he leave his busy position behind to come to a ceremony that had no direct bearing on the federal government?

When the cemetery commissioners learned of Lincoln's probable acceptance of the invitation, one of them, Commissioner Clark Carr of Illinois, suggested asking him to speak at the event. This was met with some concern, and set off a firestorm of debate among the commissioners. Some worried his remarks would be too long, too political, or too folksy for such a solemn occasion and perhaps he should not be invited to speak. Because Everett's remarks were expected to be extensive, Wills and the others did not want the ceremony to drag on too long. They also worried because Lincoln faced a grinding campaign for re-election the following year, he might use the forum for a political speech to gain a leg up. Some were concerned because

Edwin Stanton was a distinguished lawyer when President James Buchanan tapped him to be his attorney general. Lincoln later appointed him to the all-important post of secretary of war, where he was highly effective in mobilizing the North's resources to claim final victory over the South. Although he planned Lincoln's itinerary to Gettysburg, he declined to make the journey. (loc)

of Lincoln's propensity for storytelling, sometimes appropriate, sometimes not. Finally, none could recall Lincoln ever giving a speech to consecrate a cemetery. Could he find the appropriate words? In the end, the commissioners agreed to invite Lincoln to give some "short" remarks. Such a role would not require a long speech and Wills's statement was probably meant to help Lincoln better understand his role and free him from the worry of crafting a long speech taking time the president could not spare.

Wills drafted a second invitation to Lincoln on November 14: "I am authorized by the governors of the different States to invite you to be present and to participate in these ceremonies, which will doubtless be very imposing and solemnly impressive. It is the desire that, after the oration, you, as Chief Executive of the nation, formally set apart these grounds to their sacred use by a few appropriate remarks." Wills concluded the messages with an invitation to spend the night at his home along with Edward Everett and Gov. Curtin as he expected the town would be "crowded and in confusion." If Lincoln was not available to consecrate the cemetery, Wills hoped Secretary of State William Seward would do the honors and he asked him to do just that on the same day he wrote his second note to Lincoln.

A series of disappointments visited Wills a few weeks before the consecration ceremony. Several invitees begged off, including several military leaders. Maj. Gen. George Meade, the commander of the Army of the Potomac, wrote, "none can have a deeper interest in your good work than comrades in arms," but "this army has duties to perform which will not [permit me to be] . . . represented on the occasion." The nation's most honored soldier, Winfield Scott, also informed Wills that "on account of infirmities [I would] never again . . . participate in any public meeting or entertainment." Rear Admiral Charles Stewart was a no show because he received the invitation *after* the event.

The event was clearly important to Lincoln and he encouraged attendance by his Cabinet secretaries. Most found excuses to miss the ceremony. This included his two most troublesome assistants, Treasury Secretary Salmon Chase and Secretary of War Edwin Stanton. The former wrote to Wills that his "imperative public duties make it impossible for me to be present."

Wills could not worry about those absent from the ceremony as he expected an impressive array of dignitaries, including governors from the states/commonwealths of Pennsylvania, Ohio, Indiana, and New York and Cabinet members Secretary of State William Seward, Secretary of the Interior John Usher, and Postmaster General Montgomery Blair.

Lincoln's presence was actually not a foregone conclusion until a few days before the ceremony. As war-time president, Lincoln was responsible for a myriad of every-day activities and there were special responsibilities, such as providing Congress with his annual message, due on December 8. He also wrestled with a proclamation

The Eagle Hotel was a favorite spot for guests visiting Gettysburg. John Buford first used it as his headquarters during the Gettysburg campaign, and Ward Lamon and Benjamin French used it when they visited Gettysburg to inspect the cemetery and the route to it. (achs)

With her son, Tad, ill, Mary Lincoln vehemently demanded that the president not leave for Gettysburg. This graphic also shows eldest son Robert and a painting of the deceased middle son, Willie. (loc)

of amnesty and reconstruction. Lincoln took his responsibilities as commander-in-chief very seriously and his Army of the Potomac was still maneuvering to corner Robert E. Lee's army in mid-November. Andrew Curtin met with Lincoln on November 14—shortly after he was reelected to the governorship of Pennsylvania. It is probable Lincoln finally decided to attend on November 15 and the wheels were put in motion.

The trip to Gettysburg would be unprecedented in Lincoln's years as president. He otherwise never left Washington to give such a speech. So why did he go? Neither Lincoln nor his close associates ever specifically stated a rationale, but there were probably several prompts. Lincoln visited the Antietam battlefield the year before and it is fairly clear he wanted an opportunity to visit this second field of battle on Northern soil. The trip to the consecration ceremony would provide that opportunity. Lincoln's decision to wage total war to keep the Union together meant the death and maiming of thousands of young men and many more grieving family members. Lincoln sought ways to honor these men and this event did just that, and so much more. It allowed him to explain why this field of battle and all others were such an important sacrifice—that the men had not died in vain.

Lincoln also faced a tough re-election campaign, where the continuation of the war would be a major campaign issue. Lincoln needed Pennsylvania's 26 electoral votes and could not afford to alienate Gov. Curtin. After New York went Democratic, Pennsylvania became the largest Republican state in the Union. There was also the opportunity to spend some quality time with Curtin's immediate family. Gov. Curtin told Lincoln he was bringing his wife and son and may have presented it as an opportunity for the president to do the same. Indeed, several newspapers reported Lincoln intended to make the trip with his wife and, possibly, son Tad. Excursions out of Washington with his family were a rarity and Lincoln could possibly have used the ceremony to accomplish this desire.

Maj. Gen. Darius Couch had a distinguished career in the Army of the Potomac, rising to lead the II Corps. He quit after Chancellorsville rather than continue to serve under army commander Maj. Gen. Joseph Hooker, and was tapped to lead Pennsylvania's Department of the Susquehanna. (loc)

The consecration ceremony was also a once in a lifetime event. David Wills hyped it in a newspaper interview, noting it would be "one of the grandest and most imposing affairs ever beheld in the United States." This caused thousands to make the arduous trip to Gettysburg, including Lincoln and many other distinguished figures of the time. Lincoln encouraged an old business associate to travel to Gettysburg to attend the event because it "will be an interesting ceremony."

The train schedule almost undid Lincoln's plans. Because Lincoln had not decided whether he would visit Gettysburg until very close to November 19, his aides had to scramble to line up trains. The travel arrangements did not begin until Monday, November 16 when he asked Edwin Stanton to take an active role in working with the railroads to determine a workable schedule. Getting to Gettysburg was no easy matter as there were three legs to the journey, each involving a different railroad line. The presidential entourage would first board a coach on the Baltimore and Ohio Railroad bound for Baltimore. Once there, Lincoln's train would be transferred to the Northern Central Railroad. This train headed nonstop to Hanover Junction, still about 30 miles from Lincoln's destination. Here Lincoln would detrain and board a special

Pennsylvanian John Forney, who was instrumental in recommending Ward Lamon to David Wills and the rest of the planning committee, had been a clerk of the U. S. House of Representatives and was serving as secretary of the U. S. Senate at the time. These posts gave him considerable political clout. (loc)

Like John Forney, Judge Joseph Casey was another promoter of Ward Lamon and a good friend of Abraham Lincoln. Lincoln appointed him to the Federal Court of Claims, and this letter from Casey to Lincoln on January 8, 1861, recommends Simon Cameron as a Cabinet member. Lincoln complied, appointing Cameron as his first secretary of war. (loc)

train on the Hanover Junction, Hanover, and Gettysburg Railroad.

Stanton assumed Lincoln wanted to be away from Washington for a limited time, so he worked out a one-day journey that had him leaving Union Station at 6 a.m. on November 19 and would have him back to the Capitol by midnight on the same day. Stanton knew the importance Lincoln placed on touring the battlefield and he assured the president the train would arrive in Gettysburg by noon "thus giving two hours to view the ground before the dedication ceremony."

The compressed schedule troubled Lincoln and he informed Stanton of his concerns. "I do not like this arrangement," he wrote, "I do not wish to so go that by the slightest accident we fail entirely, and, at best, the whole to be a mere breathless running of the gauntlet." Lincoln's concerns were probably generated by Ward Lamon who had recently completed the difficult journey. Stanton reworked the itinerary and brought it to Lincoln. It had the president leaving Washington at noon on November 18 and returning on the evening of the following day, at the conclusion of the ceremony. Lincoln readily agreed to this schedule and disseminated it to his aides and cabinet members.

Tad Lincoln was ill on November 17, and this also delayed Lincoln's final decision to travel to Gettysburg. The death of his son, Willie, barely a year and a half before (February 1862), shook Lincoln, but not nearly as much as his wife, Mary. Not only would they not make the trip, but Mary made it clear to Lincoln that his presence was required at Tad's bedside. The compelling pull of the Gettysburg consecration ceremony ultimately won and Lincoln sustained the wrath of his wife when he informed her of his decision.

The stage was now set for the epic journey to Gettysburg.

Getting to Gettysburg

As many as 15,000 spectators ventured to Gettysburg for the consecration ceremony. Like Lincoln, they understood the significant nature of the event and wanted to be a part of history. The presence of the president only heightened their interest. A majority of the crowd hailed from the south-central Pennsylvania region, making their journey fairly easy.

Most of those venturing from distant corners of the Union were forced to rely on the already heavily used "public" transportation. An unknown woman from Philadelphia explained, "from the first day that this project had been discussed . . . I had felt as if I must be in Gettysburg whenever the ceremonies did take place." She did not realize how taxing the journey would be. After leaving Philadelphia on November 17, the train halted at Columbia, where she disembarked and made her way to a flat-bottomed boat to cross the wide Susquehanna River. The normal railroad bridge here was destroyed during the Gettysburg Campaign, forcing this work-around. She boarded another train at Wrightsville across the river, heading for York. She eventually made her way to Hanover Junction but the platform was jammed with fellow travelers and their baggage. At nightfall she boarded a converted freight car feeling "crowded, weary, and hungry. The Philadelphian

The Gettysburg railroad station has undergone extensive renovations since the battle. The tracks, which ended at the station, are now part of an extensive network. The station was significantly expanded in the 1880s. (dw)

reached Gettysburg at 11:00 p.m., where she was able to find good lodgings. This was not the case for many, as every nook and cranny, including barns, sheds, and stables, was appropriated to quarter the visitors.

The leg of the trip from Hanover Junction to Gettysburg proved to be the most challenging. A reporter from the *Cincinnati Daily Commercial* noted it was a "single thread of railroad . . . with meager rolling stock and poor management" that was expected to "convey the immense masses of people who, as early as Monday [November 16], commenced concentrating at Gettysburg." The train consisted of one passenger car and three converted freight cars, the latter without lights or heat. To make matters worse, pickpockets adept at relieving unsuspecting passengers from their belongings, plied their trade.

The railroad and the town were ill-prepared for the hordes wishing to observe the momentous consecration ceremony. According to the *Adams County Sentinel*, the influx started on Monday for the Thursday ceremony. "The trains became heavier and heavier as the day of the consecration approached." Trains arrived every few hours from Wednesday morning through Thursday morning, "swelling the crowd to immense proportions." Bands descended upon Gettysburg from many cities and towns and they made their presence felt, walking "about like roaring lions seeking whom they might serenade."

The town with a mere 2,400 people prior to the war with its four hotels struggled to accommodate the projected crush of visitors. According to Baltimore Street resident Henry Sweney, "our town roused up to action,—meetings were held and committees were appointed to wait on strangers and procure them accommodations in every house large and small, high and low. . . . Churches, public schools, town halls, all the private dwellings, barns, etc. were thrown open to receive them. Every house groaned with the good things of this life prepared to feed the coming crowd."

The town's planning activities helped prepare for the influx of visitors. Henry Sweney noted "every building public or private was filled and for miles around the town the houses were filled with the congregated throng." Another Gettysburg resident, Emily Souder, recalled "the churches were lighted and warmed for the reception of those who could not find quarters elsewhere," but still, she noted, "the streets were filled with crowds of people." Those lucky enough to find a bed, usually were forced to share it. A woman from Philadelphia recalled sleeping in a bed with four others. She was fortunate, for she recalled 17 unfortunates attempting to get comfortable on the blood-stained floor. Many were forced to take a "rigid repose in the cars or carriages," or not attempt to sleep at all and instead roam about the town all night.

Gen. James Fry was a well-regarded West Pointer who served from the War with Mexico through the Civil War and beyond. He served as provost marshal general of the United States Army during the Civil War. Fry was well-regarded by Lincoln and acted as his escort to the train station on November 18, 1863. (loc)

Those who arrived early wanted to see the battlefield, and enterprising town residents rounded up every wheeled vehicle and four-legged animal they could find. Edward Everett was one of the earliest arrivals, spending countless hours on the battlefield, attempting to gain the inspiration that would make his oration noteworthy and praiseworthy of the event. The wave of humanity taxed the town. The "Philadelphia Lady" noted "the tranquility of the little town was by this time if not before completely broken up." Toward evening she made her way to the train station. "The President was hourly looked for and the interest and excitement was great." She admitted her quest to witness the president detraining was in vain.

General James Fry of the War Department arrived at the White House on the morning of November 18 to transport Lincoln to Union Station where he would hop on a special train of the Baltimore and Ohio Railroad. Lincoln was not ready and a worried Fry sought to speed the president's preparations, lest they miss the train. Lincoln smiled and told Fry one of his many stories, this one of the man in Illinois who was being conveyed to the gallows. As spectators were hurrying past his cart, he called out, "Boys, you

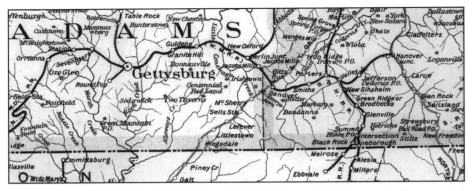

The Gettysburg Railroad Company was formed in 1851 to connect the town with the Hanover Branch Line in Hanover Junction, about 16 miles away. This provided a link to the Northern Central Railroad, leading to Philadelphia, Harrisburg, and Baltimore. The rail line to Gettysburg began service on December 16, 1858, and operated until December 31, 1942. (wp)

needn't be in such a hurry; there won't be any fun till I get there."

Lincoln was probably conflicted by the desire to stay put to take care of state business and his ailing son, and his strong desire to be present at the consecration ceremony and see the battlefield. Lincoln and his entourage boarded the train bedecked with an American flag, wreaths, and other evergreens. In addition to his personal secretaries John Hay and John Nicolay, the three cabinet secretaries, Blair, Seward, and Usher, boarded Lincoln's private train at noon. The group was joined by Edward Everett's daughter, Charlotte Wise, and son-in-law, Henry, a host of newspaper correspondents and the military guard scheduled to participate in the ceremony. Among the guests were French minister, M. Mercier and the Italian minister, M. Bertinatti, along with several aides. Relations with France were delicate, to say the least, and this journey was perhaps a way Lincoln could help cement the Union's relationship with this important ally. Lincoln was fond of the new nation of Italy and had actually offered its unifier, Giuseppe Garibaldi, a major general's commission and command of the Union armies after the Battle of First Bull Run in 1861. Garibaldi refused and the invitation may have been more of a courtesy than political expediency. According to historian Martin Johnson, whether intentional or not, "the participation of foreign dignitaries added an elevated, international, and nonpartisan tone to the president's party and was much noted in the newspapers as adding dignity and impressiveness to the occasion." The Marine Band was also on the train to provide music along the way.

Lincoln took his place at the rear of the last car so he could periodically exit and give speeches to crowds along the way. The car, provided by John Garrett, the president of the Baltimore & Ohio Railroad, was opulent—much fancier than Lincoln's tastes. Passenger Wayne McVeigh recalled, "Whenever the train stopped, Mr. Lincoln was required to address from the rear platform some words to the few people who had gathered to pay their respects to him, but I remember nothing of importance said by him on any of these occasions."

Secretary of State Seward and the president became uneasy as the train approached Baltimore. The last time Lincoln ventured through Baltimore on a train was just before his inauguration in February 1861, when plans for an assassination attempt were uncovered. A large number of citizens met Lincoln's train at Camden Station in Baltimore. The Marine Band hopped off the train to serenade Lincoln from the platform. A "considerable crowd" milled about the platform—the local newspapers carried information of Lincoln's route and itinerary. Lincoln merely waved to the crowd. Hanover Junction was the next leg of the trip, but the Baltimore & Ohio did not make this journey. Instead, horses were hooked to each of the cars and they were dragged across town to Bolton Station of the Northern Central Railroad. About 200 people were waiting for Lincoln, but he was in no mood to make speeches or small talk until Secretary Seward encouraged him to make an appearance. He did so, shaking hands and kissing babies.

The journey continued at 2:00 p.m., this time with a baggage car added at the end of the train to serve as a dining car. Lincoln spent the trip talking with others which helped make the long, wearisome trip, less so. Many on the train recalled Lincoln's ambivalence. One moment he was cracking jokes or telling humorous stories, the next he was shedding tears about sad incidents

John Garrett was President of the B & O Railroad, one of the most important lines in America during the Civil War. His opulent personal rail car provided a comfortable vehicle for Lincoln's travel to Gettysburg. (loc)

The Wills house played a prominent role in the planning and implementation of the consecration ceremony. David Wills had many meetings here, and Lincoln, Everett, and other dignities spent the night before the ceremony here. (loc)

that "deeply touched the hearts of his listeners." A passenger recalled him discussing "sacrifices of life yet to be offered" and "hearts and homes yet to be made desolate before this dreadful war, so wickedly forced upon us, is over." Lincoln left his personal car at least once to interact with others making the trip. A soldier recalled Lincoln "placed everyone who approached him at his ease." The converted baggage car attached to the rear of the train provided a lunch venue and Lincoln delighted telling stories to those who shared his repast. As the train approached Pennsylvania, an aide pointed out one of the markers designating the Mason-Dixon Line, fixed in 1767—the boundary between free- and slave-states. Lincoln looked at the stone with great interest without saying a word.

The train halted at Hanover Junction, where the cars were transferred to the Hanover Junction, Hanover, and Gettysburg Railroad for the final leg of his journey. He was to have rendezvoused at Hanover Junction with the governors of Pennsylvania, New York, Ohio, and West Virginia, but their train was delayed, so the train pulled out without these distinguished guests. The overdue train would not arrive until 11:00 p.m. Lincoln's train stopped briefly at Hanover, where a large crowd gathered "to get a good look at the President" and beckoned him from his car. According to the

Philadelphia Inquirer, Lincoln "delivered one of his brief, quaint speeches for which he is celebrated." He gave the crowd one of his standard lines: "Well, you have seen me, and according to general experience, you have seen less than you expected to see." Knowing of the large cavalry battle waged in the streets of Hanover on June 30, Lincoln asked the crowd: "You had the Rebels here last summer, hadn't you?" to which the crowd yelled, "Yes!" He then asked, "Well, did you fight them any?" According to the *Inquirer*, "This was a poser. The people looked at each other with a half-amused, half-puzzled expression." An embarrassing silence filled the space that was broken only when women approached Lincoln with bouquets of flowers and a beautiful handmade flag.

Lincoln's six-hour journey to Gettysburg finally ended between 6:00 and 6:30 p.m. when the train pulled into the fairly new railway station on Carlisle Street. A horde of people was on hand to greet him. David Wills, with Edward Everett and Ward Lamon in tow, pushed their way through the crowd to meet Lincoln and the group walked one block south to the Square. Lincoln met them with a "weary smile" and Seward wearing an "essentially bad hat." So many people crowded the platform and streets that "the president was extracted from the good natured pressure, with some difficulty."

The crowd eagerly followed Lincoln and his entourage one block to the Wills home on the Square. Here he was introduced to Mrs. Catherine ("Jennie") Wills, eight months pregnant, and was then shown to his bedroom on the second floor, facing the Square. He was joined in the room by William Johnson, a black man whom Lincoln had befriended many years before and who served as his personal groom during the trip. Lincoln may have winced when noting the bed was too short to accommodate his 6'4" frame, but he probably welcomed the two tables. A chair accompanied one of the tables—perfect for completing his address. The other held a washbasin and pitcher of cold water which he probably used to wash his face and

David Wills not only served as host and organizer of the event, he also opened his home to guests and the general public who would visit Lincoln and Curtin after the consecration ceremony. (gnmp)

As the wife of David Wills, Catherine Wills played host to more than 30 guests in her home on November 18, 1863. The mother of three children, she was expecting another during this period. (gnmp)

hands. A bureau, two rocking chairs, and a wardrobe completed the room's furnishings. Sgt. Hugh Paxton Bigham of the 21st Pennsylvania Cavalry was detailed to guard his door and his younger brother, Rush, manned the front door. Indeed, the entire Company B of the six-month regiment composed of local young men provided the guard. A local newspaper claimed "much of the good order that characterized our town both night and day" was due to these men.

Lincoln then headed downstairs where Mrs. Wills prepared a sumptuous dinner for the president and 25 others. Wills placed the president at the head of the table

The mile-long bridge spanning the mighty Susquehanna River between Columbia and Wrightsville, Pennsylvania, was vitally important to units of Gen. Jubal Early's Confederate division attempting to capture Harrisburg, Pennsylvania's capital. Pennsylvania militia set the bridge on fire as Georgia troops prepared to cross, depriving the Confederates of a direct avenue to Harrisburg. (hw)

with Everett to his right. Everett, who imagined Lincoln to be a boorish Westerner, soon engaged him in a lively conversation and would later share the impression of Lincoln being "the peer of any man at the table" in "gentlemanly appearance, manners, and conversation."

Lincoln was interrupted several times during the early evening. The dinner gathering could hear the music of the 5th New York Artillery Band perched in front of the Wills house to serenade the president. A male quartet also began singing several songs, and then broke into "We are coming, Father Abraham, three hundred thousand strong." These performances acted as a magnet and the crowd grew to an immense size. Lincoln and others trying to enjoy their evening meal could easily hear the music and commotion outside, and soon the crowd began chanting "continuously and vociferously" for the president to emerge and address them.

Giving in to their demands, Lincoln rose from the table and headed to the front door where he bowed and waved to the crowd. Jacob Hoke recalled "the appearance of the President was the

signal for an outburst of enthusiasm that I had never heard equaled. While the people cheered and otherwise expressed their delight, he stood before us bowing his acknowledgments. At length silence was restored, when his face relaxed its appearance of careworn sadness and anxiety, and a kind of genial smile overspread his countenance."

A voice yelled out for a speech and others joined in. Lincoln complied with a rambling speech that disappointed many who heard it:

I appear before you, fellow citizens, merely to thank you for this compliment. The inference is a very fair one that you would hear me for a little while at least, were I to commence to make a speech. I do not appear before you for the purpose of doing so, and for several substantial reasons. The most substantial of these is that I have no speech to make. In my position it is somewhat important that I should not say any foolish thing. It very often happens that the only way to help it is to say nothing at all. Believing that is my present condition this evening, I must beg of you to excuse me from addressing you further.

A reporter caught up with the spirit of the crowd noted, "He said nothing, but he said it well." A local newspaper noted, "He made but a few remarks, but they were characteristic of the pure and honest President." John Hay, Lincoln's personal aide, recorded in his diary the president,

Like many 19th Century towns, Gettysburg boasted a center square, called the "Diamond." It has gone through many permutations, including a large steel structure in 1886. The site has been used for a variety of community events. This photo shows the arrival of the new Sibley Steam Fire Engine in 1886. (achs)

The Gettysburg Railroad station's Italianate style was popular when it was built in 1859. Guests arriving via train walked through the station to reach Carlisle Street, which would take them to the Diamond or Washington Hotel across the street. (achs)

"said half a dozen words meaning nothing & went in." Many in the crowd expected Lincoln to mourn with those who had lost a loved one and console them, to inspire the soldiers to fight on, and to honor the dead. Lincoln did none of this. Perhaps he was excessively tired from his long trip, a bit apprehensive about the morrow, and conflicted about being away from Washington. Historian Martin Johnson also explained that had Lincoln uttered the words and sentiments the audience craved "he would not have been Lincoln . . . it was just [not] his personality."

When Lincoln slipped back into the Wills house, the disappointed crowd headed next door to Robert Harper's home. Both homes "were adorned with flags, wreaths and evergreens in honor of the occasion and as a mark of respect for the illustrious visitor," according to the *Franklin Repository*. Harper was the editor of the *Adams County Sentinel* and the gracious host of a number of luminaries, such as Secretary of State Seward and Benjamin French. Seward emerged during the serenade and gave a short, impassioned speech on the role of the South and slavery in causing this terrible conflict and he paid tribute to those who had fought and died in the fields around Gettysburg. Former Congressman Edward McPherson followed Seward with comments from the steps of the Harper home. The crowd next moved south to the David Buehler home and egged remarks out of Postmaster General Montgomery Blair. Sensing there were more speeches to be had, the crowd next moved to the Fahnestock home where newspaper publisher John Forney and Wayne McVeagh, an influential member of the Republican Party, were induced to provide remarks to the crowd. It was certainly a night to remember.

Charles Mason and Jeremiah Dixon resolved the boundary dispute between Maryland and Pennsylvania by conducting an extensive survey between 1763 and 1767. Markers were placed every five miles along the line bearing the family coat of arms (Penn Family in Pennsylvania and Calvert Family in Maryland). (achs)

Lincoln peeled himself from the dining room table between 9-10 p.m. to return to his room and continue drafting his consecration remarks. William Johnson appeared barely ten minutes later, as Lincoln requested an audience with Wills. According to an affidavit signed in 1894, Wills recalled Lincoln saying that "he had just seated himself to put upon paper a few thoughts for the to-morrow's exercises, and had sent for me to ascertain what part he was to take in them, and what was expected of him." Wills went into detail about the morrow's ceremony and then excused himself.

The Hanover Junction Railroad depot was the starting/ending point of the Gettysburg Railroad. The depot exists in good condition to this day. (loc)

Wayne McVeagh was district attorney of Chester County, Pennsylvania, during the Civil War. He took time away from his office to serve in the Pennsylvania militia when Robert E. Lee invaded the North in 1862 and 1863. (loc)

Gettysburg resident Robert Harper inherited the *Gettysburg Sentinel* from his father and was its publisher until the paper merged with another in 1867. A strong Republican, Harper opened his home to guests during the cemetery's consecration celebration. (achs)

William Johnson again appeared at about 11:00 p.m., with a second request for an audience with Lincoln. This time Lincoln wanted to see Seward. Wills offered to bring Seward to his home, but Lincoln wanted to visit him, so Wills and Sgt. Bingham led him to Harper's home next door. The Union Glee Club of Philadelphia watched Lincoln emerge and immediately broke into song. Lincoln and Seward conferred for about half an hour, presumably about the speech and plans for visiting the battlefield prior to the ceremony. Lincoln then emerged from the home and the crowd requested another speech. Lincoln told them they would get their wish tomorrow: "I can't speak tonight," he said, "I will see you all tomorrow. Good night." The night was dark and the crowd immense so Lincoln asked Sgt. Bingham to lead the way back to the Wills house. "You clear the way and I will hold on to your coat," he said. He added that "It was quite dark, but we got through nicely."

Sometime that evening, a welcome telegram arrived from Washington with the comforting news that his son Tad was feeling better. Sgt. Bingham recalled Lincoln reappearing at the door of his room and telling him, "This telegram was from home. My little boy has been very sick, but he is better."

David Wills was in for a long night as the tardy train carrying Gov. Curtin and the other governors did not arrive until after midnight. The Wills home was packed with guests, Everett recalled: 38 were lodged there, forcing some creativity. Wills approached Everett, who recounted that Wills "proposed to put the Governor into bed with me." Everett's bladder issues, coupled with his station in life, caused him to put up a fuss, and he continued that Curtin, "kindly went out and found a lodging elsewhere." Curtin paid his respects to Lincoln before he left and saw him sitting at his bedroom table engrossed in preparing his speech. Everett's daughter Charlotte was not so fortunate. She shared a bed with two other women, and when the bed broke, all rolled onto the floor.

It was now past midnight and Lincoln may have made some additional modifications to his speech after conferring with Seward. He was probably very tired as the long and emotional day had taken its toll and he decided to turn in for the night. The crowds outside his window remained large and boisterous. Many recalled the difficulty in getting to sleep that night, mostly from the sounds of the rambunctious crowd milling about the Square and spilling into the adjoining streets. A reporter wondered whether it was "the want of sleeping quarters: or an "irrepressible enthusiasm" that kept people in the streets. The streets remained filled when the first light illuminated November 19.

The Big Day Arrives

CHAPTER EIGHT

November 19, 1863

November 19 dawned bright and warm—unusual for mid-November. Resident Henry Jacobs noted the temperature reached 52 degrees during the day, which was "just warm enough to prevent a chill, and yet cool enough to be slightly bracing." Trains continued pulling into the depot, carrying additional observers of the day's special event, but most seemed to be "coming in every direction, and in every avenue of approach, on foot, in carriages and on horseback," according to Emily Souder. Jacob Hoke believed "the whole population of the surrounding country seems to be crowding into Gettysburg." A reporter for the *Washington Daily Morning Chronicle* wrote "All was hubbub and confusion." The editor of the *Gettysburg Complier* observed, "The streets swarmed with people from all sections of the Union, the number variously estimated from twenty to fifty thousand." The actual number was 10,000-15,000, which was still an immense gathering in a town ill-equipped to handle such an explosion of guests. The crowd was so big, the *Adams County Sentinel* reported, "Every available spot on the principal streets was occupied."

Lincoln awoke early. A young woman living about a block from the Wills house ventured to the square to see the growing crowd. Looking up at the Wills house, she could see Lincoln pacing his room as though "engaged in deep thought."

David Wills and Ward Lamon precisely planned how the various groups forming the procession would form on the three streets leading to the Diamond and the order they would march in to the cemetery. (loc)

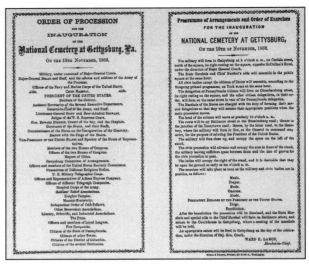

Both Lincoln and Everett wanted to see the battlefield, but went their separate ways. Everett, accompanied by several men from Massachusetts, took a leisurely walk around the near-fringes of the battlefield. Lincoln borrowed a spring-less buckboard and with Seward, headed west to see the scene of the first day's battle where Maj. Gen. John Reynolds had surrendered his life to preserve the Union. Curtin, still weary from his late-night arrival, spent a comfortable morning chatting with David Wills about a variety of topics relating to the cemetery and interment of the dead.

Lincoln's selection of the first day's battlefield was probably not just expedient. He knew General John Reynolds, invited him to the White House, and asked him to assume command of the Army of the Potomac. Reynolds demurred, wanting full control of the army—something Lincoln was unwilling to relinquish. Now he wanted to see where a sniper's bullet had cut down one of his most valued leaders.

Although the battlefield had essentially healed, the signs of battle remained easy to see. Lincoln probably returned from his battlefield visit profoundly affected by what he observed.

Upon his return to the Wills house, Lincoln dressed for the ceremony and then went down to breakfast, where he requested a cup of tea. He left the table about 9:00 a.m. and returned to his room, where he sat down again with his speech. His visit to the battlefield may have caused him to modify some of the passages. John Nicolay reported for duty and found Lincoln at the small desk with the speech in front of him and a pencil in his hand.

Lamon had shown himself to be an able organizer, considering every detail of the event. He spent much of the evening before discussing roles and responsibilities with his marshals and he was ready as the morning sun filled the sky. Lamon could not know his timetable would go awry from the start due to the size of the crowd. The procession was scheduled to step off at 10:00 a.m., but because all were to march to the cemetery, it would begin later.

Lincoln emerged from the Wills home just before 10:00 a.m. wearing his customary black Prince Albert coat and stove-pipe hat, wrapped in a mourning band. He added the band to mourn his dead son, but today it would extend to the thousands who had died in battle. He carried white riding gloves as he headed for the street and the awaiting mount. Most agreed Lincoln seemed sad and pensive. His mood quickly changed when the crowd ignited in cheers and applause. A newspaper reported Lincoln was "half blushing amid the intense ardor" and a resident of the area recorded in her diary, "Such a homage I never saw or imagined could be shown to any one person, as the people bestow upon Lincoln." The Commissioners' gamble to invite Lincoln to speak was paying off.

The horse assigned to Lincoln has been vigorously debated by those who penned their observations of the event. Several claimed seeing Lincoln mounting a small horse. One recalled it was a "small, fat horse known as a Dutch horse . . . His feet almost touched the ground." Another added that it was "laughable to see the president himself astride a small mount, with his long legs almost touching the ground." One posited, "In case the steed became fractious it looked as though the President could simply plant his feet on the ground and let it pass from under." Those who observed this unusual pairing thought it because of Lincoln's poor horsemanship.

Henry Jacobs was an 18-year-old resident of Gettysburg during the battle. He remained at home and witnessed the retreat of the Union troops, the entry of Confederate troops, and Pickett's Charge (from his roof). He became a noted theologian and rose to the presidency of a seminary. (achs)

Pennsylvanian and West Point graduate John Reynolds rose to the rank of major general command of the I Corps at Gettysburg. His was the first infantry to engage the Confederates on the morning of July 1. (loc)

John Reynolds was killed near Herbst Woods as the Iron Brigade went into action against James Archer's Brigade. The Lancaster native was held in high esteem by Lincoln and many of his military comrades. Lincoln had offered him command of the Army of the Potomac, but he turned it down because he realized he would have little autonomy. (lg)

Others claimed the mount was of normal size, sleek, and befitting a president. Perhaps to bridge the difference, one observer recalled the president beginning the ride on a small horse, but a "handsome sorrel charger was found [and Lincoln] was given a better mount half-way through." None of the contemporary accounts of the ceremony in letter or newspaper ever mentioned Lincoln's horse. Given the close scrutiny of the president, one would believe such a humorous and noteworthy event would have been described. Legend has it that the horse was selected by John McClellan, who owned the hotel across the street. An accomplished expert on horseflesh, McClellan purportedly selected a superb horse discarded during the Gettysburg campaign because of a severe saddle sore, but now completely healed. Indeed, Henry Sweney wrote ten days after the ceremony that Lincoln was "mounted on a beautiful bay charger."

Lincoln's horsemanship abilities may have a bearing on the story. Some observers, particularly those witnessing a small horse, commented on Lincoln's poor horsemanship, noting how he swayed side to side and almost fell off, but others observed an accomplished rider. A reporter noted, "I must do the President justice to say that his awkwardness, which is so often remarked, does not extend to his horsemanship." It is probable that Lincoln was an average horseman who was given a good steed at the start of the procession.

Getting to the horse proved to be more difficult than Lincoln or Lamon anticipated as the crowd surged forward as he emerged from the Wills house, engulfing him, requesting handshakes, touching his clothing, and cheering his very presence. Lamon, with the help of some of his marshals, interceded and helped Lincoln push through the throng. Lincoln quickly mounted his horse but the crowd again surged forward. Lamon understood the danger of this situation so he ordered his marshals to disperse the crowd and at least create a buffer around the president. An observer noted the marshals, "having mercy on his oft-wrung arm and weary exertions, caused the crowd to desist and allow the president to sit in peace upon his horse. But the people were not yet satisfied, must have another three cheers for honest Old Abe, and they fairly eclipsed the others." Lincoln was now joined by his cabinet members who would ride with him.

The marshals' most challenging task was probably assembling the citizens from the 18 states that had lost sons in the fight. Many chose not to march, but watched along the parade route or arrived in front of the ceremonial platform well in advance of the procession to secure a good place. This led historian William Barton to muse, "While the procession was not all that

This 1863 image of Baltimore Street is facing south, away from the Diamond. John Schick's store, which became a warehouse for the Christian Commission, can be seen on the right. (achs)

a procession might have been, there was a procession of a sort." John Hay, Lincoln's secretary, was less charitable about Lamon's efforts of organizing the procession, noting the "procession formed itself in an orphanly sort of way, and moved out with very little help from anybody." Those civilians who marched in the procession lined up by state and one newspaper man tried to quantify the number of each, noting that Pennsylvania provided the largest number of citizens, followed by Ohio, Wisconsin, and then Massachusetts.

Leading the procession down Baltimore Street the Marine Band followed by military units "rolled on as waves of the ocean." The 2nd United States Artillery followed the band, and then the U.S. Regular Cavalry, Gen. Couch and his staff and the president and his entourage. David Wills shepherded the state agents and Curtin took care of the dozen or so other current, past, or recently elected governors. A newspaper reported, "in the procession to the Cemetery were long glittering lines of troops, headed by Generals with dashing staffs and interspersed with scarlet-colored and plumed bands, and groups of civilians, regiments of Odd Fellows and masons with their gay trappings, all moving to the sound of cannon from that knob of Cemetery Hill."

The procession down Baltimore Street was to include everyone who was making their way to the cemetery, but many chose to watch the column file past. This view is looking toward the Diamond, and the soldiers' muskets are easily seen at the front of the column. (loc)

All eyes were on Lincoln. A Chicagoan recalled Lincoln was "by far the most striking man in that great cavalcade of distinguished men." Another observer noted Lincoln "rode easily, bowing to the right and left" as he headed toward the cemetery, and another recalled, "His deeply cut features looked hard and worn." A Pittsburgh reporter sadly wrote, "He looks much older than when we last saw him, two years ago." Those spectators lining the streets put up quite a cheer as Lincoln rode past. He was hard to miss. "He towered above everyone, and his gigantic proportions seemed to be magnified by the shape of the odd high silk hat that he wore," noted a resident long after the event.

It must have been a thrilling sight for Lincoln to ride into the cemetery's entrance on Taneytown Road lined by soldiers standing at "present arms." The makings of the cemetery were easy to see. "The graves are fresh, for they are newly made," noted a reporter, "marked as yet, at head and foot, only by bits of board stuck in the ground."

The head of the procession reached the platform at about 11:15 a.m. where Lincoln and the rest of the distinguished guests dismounted and climbed the steps to the three-foot high platform at the left-front of the stage. David Wills was waiting on stage and escorted each of the front-row guests to his seat. The newspapers reported Lincoln was received "with the respect and perfect silence" appropriate to "the solemnity of the occasion." Lincoln occupied the seat of honor in the middle of the first row. A seat for Edward Everett was reserved on Lincoln's right, but

This view of Gettysburg from the roof of the Evergreen Cemetery Gatehouse on Cemetery Hill shows Baltimore Pike in the foreground and a militia encampment on the right of the photo. Alexander Gardner took this photograph on July 7, 1863. (loc)

the great orator was nowhere to be seen. He was in the tent reserved for him behind the stage. Two clergymen sat on Everett's right, Baugher and then Stockton, followed by Benjamin French and William Saunders.

Sec. of State Seward occupied the chair to Lincoln's left. Three of the governors were seated to Seward's left: Curtin (Pennsylvania), Tod (Ohio), and Seymour (New York). Other governors, military leaders, Everett's daughter, the foreign dignitaries, and other special guests occupied the two rows of seats behind the front row. Gov. Tod, described as "good-humored, florid, and plump," was a strong Lincoln ally who wholeheartedly supported the cemetery, so his place was secure as a representative of the Republican governors. Wills and the Commission needed balance, so they seated a Democratic governor, Horatio Seymour of New York, next to Tod. Seymour, described as a "stout, hearty, well-to-do man," was also a prime candidate to head the Democratic ticket in next year's presidential election. He had a decidedly cool relationship with Lincoln as they had clashed over the draft, which had caused widespread rioting in New York City.

Master of Ceremonies Hugh Lamon occupied a seat near the steps on the far left of the stage. Already behind schedule, he was probably displeased by Everett's absence. The bands took turns playing music while all awaited the main speaker. Everett finally appeared, slowly walking from the tent to steps leading to the top of the platform, guided by Wills and Seymour. Once on stage, the 70-year-old moved slowly to his chair, where he was greeted by the president.

The ceremony would now commence. No one seemed to care that it was well behind schedule.

Edward McPherson was a two-term Congressman and newspaper editor who owned a farm just west of Gettysburg that was the scene of heavy fighting on the first day's battle. (achs)

The Consecration Ceremony and the Remainder of the Day

CHAPTER NINE

November 19, 1863

The front door to David Wills's house saw a plethora of activities around the time of the Soldiers' National Cemetery Consecration. Lincoln used this door to enter and leave the home, and he greeted people at the doorway after the ceremony. (lg)

As Edward Everett settled into his chair, Ward Lamon stepped to the front of the stage and welcomed the audience and read the regret notes of those unable to join the event. Benjamin French then motioned for Birgfield's band to play a dirge entitled "Homage d'un Heros." Reporters later called it "magnificent," a "piece eloquently suited for the occasion," and "performed with pre-eminent skills." The sounds bathed the large crowd but elicited little applause, possibly because most believed it inappropriate to clap for funeral-like music. The prayers and speeches would now follow. Despite the *New York Times* reporter's claim that "So quiet were the people that every word uttered by the orator of the day must have been heard by them all, notwithstanding the immensity of the concourse." Other reporters disagreed. For example, the reporter from the *Indianapolis Daily Journal* noted, "I couldn't hear one word. Nor did one-tenth of the crowd. But it is no matter; it will be published." Obviously, the location of the listener dictated the degree to which they could hear the speeches.

It was now Rev. Thomas Stockton's moment for his Invocation. A reporter for the *Cincinnati Daily Commercial* described Stockton as possessing a "most unearthly face out of the grave; absolutely colorless; the lips as white as the basted cheek, and the flowing hair, and tuft of whiskers under the chin as snowy

Although a Democrat, David Tod was a strong supporter of Lincoln, but because of his tepid support for the abolition of slavery, he was not nominated for a second term. Lincoln offered him a position in his administration, but he rejected it because of poor health. (loc)

Fifty-three-year-old Horatio Seymour was serving his second term as New York's governor during the battle of Gettysburg. A Democrat, he opposed Lincoln and many of his policies, including the draft. (loc)

white as wool." The Invocation ran long for an opening prayer, causing John Hay to quip it was "a prayer which thought it was an oration." It was in fact four times longer than Lincoln's upcoming address. A reporter called Stockton's remarks "eloquent" and the passionate remarks, ending with the Lord's Prayer, purportedly brought tears to many in the audience. A reporter for the *Adams County Sentinel* reported, "The President evidently felt deeply, and with the venerable statesman and patriot, Hon. Edward Everett, who was by his side, seemed not ashamed to let their sympathetic tears be seen."

The Marine Band next struck up Luther's hymn, "Old Hundred" in what a newspaper reporter called "all its grand and sublime beauty." The hymn was wildly popular during this era, "probably played and sung more than any other hymn," according to a period historian. The Marines did not disappoint. The *Washington Daily Morning Chronicle* claimed it was played "with great effect, in all its grand and sublime beauty."

Lamon again returned to center stage to introduce the main speaker. Edward Everett vied with Lincoln as being the ceremony's most anticipated speaker. The crowd watched as Everett slowly rose and shuffled to the front of the stage. The *Cincinnati Daily Commercial* described Everett as possessing a "head white with the snows of seventy winters, but his form as erect, his eye as bright, his complexion as clear, his voice as full and sweet, his gesture as graceful and the expression of his face as genial as in his manhood's prime." Austin Bierbower recalled long after the speech: "I was struck with his appearance—a large man with white head and face, looking the typical statesman and gentleman of the old school."

Those commenting on Everett's delivery and substance of the speech were impressed. He was complimented for his "clear voice." Bierbower recalled Everett "stood erect and spoke with a deep, resonant voice." Another recalled "every word is faithfully memorized; there is no hesitation; the

This photo shows the raised platform party on the left and the tall flagpole on the right. The boys in the foreground probably knew it was a big event, but probably grew bored and hung out behind the crowd. (loc)

stream of eloquence flows steadily on . . . Though his discourse was probably written out, he delivered it so naturally that he seemed to be speaking extemporaneously. He spoke slowly and appeared to deliberate on each sentence. The grace and beauty of his delivery and of the language impressed me more than did his thought, which was not much above the commonplace."

The title of the oration was "The Battles of Gettysburg" and Everett opened his remarks by comparing this ceremony with the rites performed at Marathon for the Greek heroes who had halted the Persian invasion. He spent the remaining two hours recounting the events culminating with the Gettysburg fight and its seminal events. He also provided an accounting of the crimes committed by the South against the United States that amounted to treason. Knowing the end of his speech was near, Everett dramatically expounded his last paragraph:

Surely I would do no injustice to the other noble achievements of the war, which have reflected such honor on both arms of the service, and have entitled the armies and the navy of the United States, their officers and men, to the warmest thanks and the richest rewards which a grateful people can pay. But they, I am sure, will join us in saying, as we bid farewell to the dust of these martyr-heroes, that wheresoever throughout the civilized world the accounts of this great warfare are read, and down to the latest period of recorded time, in the glorious annals of our common country, there will be no brighter page than that which relates The Battles of Gettysburg.

Everett's remarks collected a variety of viewpoints. One reporter declared it was "for beauty of language, terseness of statement, and a certain stational and formal eloquence, is unsurpassed by any previous effort of his life." Wayne MacVeagh, Lincoln's guest on the train, called it, "perfectly adapted to the occasion, and exactly what such an oration ought to be. It was of necessity elaborate and long, because it involved a complete justification of the war then in progress and a graphic and detailed description of the battle which had been so recently fought where we were standing; but it was eminently, scholarly, and eloquent." Benjamin French agreed, writing in his diary that it was "one of the greatest, most eloquent, elegant, and appropriate orations to which I ever listened. I stood at his very side, through it, and I think the oratory could not be surpassed by mortal man."

Others were disappointed. One called it "smooth and cold," but lacking "one stirring thought, one vivid picture, one thrilling appeal." Another thought it "painfully cold . . . with no sunbeam warmth. He seemed the hired mourner—the laureate chanting

This photo helps give perspective on the location of the platform. The Evergreen Cemetery Gatehouse and tall flagpole can be seen to the left. The platform is just right of center, and next to it is Edward Everett's tent. (loc)

This remarkable photo shows Lincoln on the platform surrounded by a number of dignitaries. Men wearing white sashes were marshals. It is possible that Ward Lamon and Benjamin French are in the right of the photo, both wearing sashes. (loc)

a funeral dirge to order." Many modern historians believe Everett's oration missed the mark in content and delivery. Frank Klement wrote, "Everett's speech did not scour. It was too long . . . recited without emotion or imagination."

How did the audience respond to Everett's two-hour oration? The *Baltimore Sun* and *New York Times* reported his remarks were "listened to with marked attention." This may have been true of the first hour, but as the second droned on, many listeners on the fringes wandered off to visit the cemetery or simply talk with friends. They pinned their hopes on a good speech by their president.

Everett ended his remarks with a flourish eliciting a smattering of applause. Lincoln's actions during the long speech are in doubt. Some believed Lincoln listened intently throughout the speech, but Gettysburg Lutheran Pastor Junius Remensnyder recalled Lincoln "seemed to grow quite weary, and almost acted as if he were bored. He twisted his gaunt form and his long limbs in every direction." Secretary Seward, hat pulled down over his eyes to ward off the sun, sat with his arms folded. An observer noted Seward had "grown old fast." Reverend Stockton sat "impassively." A less than charitable modern

This is a close-up of the prior photo showing a hatless Lincoln looking down. He is clearly the center of attention. (loc)

historian thought the applause "was given by those who were glad the oration was finally over." Lincoln warmly reached over and clasped Everett's hand in appreciation at the conclusion of the oration.

Lamon now motioned for the twelve members of the Baltimore Glee Club to chant French's ode. The ode "elicited the admiration of all," re-energizing the crowd and preparing them for the "minor" speaker. Up to this point, the crowd vacillated between wishing to show appreciation to the speaker and exhibiting a solemn air. The latter tended to prevail. Now, the audience erupted in thunderous applause. Benjamin French could not have been more exuberant. He recorded in his diary, "I was never so flattered at any production of my own, as in relation to that same Hymn. All who heard it seemed to consider it more appropriate and most happily conceived."

Lamon now stepped forward to introduce Abraham Lincoln. Jacob Hoke remembered, "Lincoln arose, and amidst the thunder of artillery and the tremendous applause of the immense multitude, advanced to the front of the platform." This created a "rustle of expectation and a visible attempt to get nearer the stand." Possibly because of the location of the graves and a desire to hear the speeches, the crowd in front of the stand became very dense. A nurse who had taken time from her caring duties recalled all were "packed like fishes in a barrel . . . We stood, almost suffocated."

Lincoln slowly uncoiled his long frame from his uncomfortable seat and stood before the large crowd. He pulled out a pair of spectacles from his pocket and reached into another for two pages. An Ohio newspaperman closely watched Lincoln's face, noting, "It is a thoughtful, kindly, care-worn face, impassive in repose, the eyes cast down, the lids thin and firmly set, the cheeks sunken, and the whole indicating weariness, and anything but good health." Another claimed his face "was very sad, his gestures few but his voice clear as a silver toned bell." Wayne MacVeagh recalled seeing a president exhibiting "a great melancholy, [but] it was somehow lightened as by a great hope." No one could have known Lincoln was beginning to grow ill from his bout with a mild form smallpox that would confine him to bed for ten days during the latter part of the month and into December.

Lincoln waited for the commotion to subside and then "in a sharp, unmusical, and treble voice, reads the following brief and pithy." William Tipton recalled that Lincoln "looked sadly over the cemetery and after a pause began his family speech . . . in a sad voice, entirely devoid of the oratorical zeal and fire which had characterized Mr. Everett's address." Another noted other differences among the two main speakers. Lincoln's voice "was high and thin, quite in contrast with Everett's strong baritone, but it had great carrying power and could be heard to the limits of the

This closeup shows the platform to the right of the prior photos. Two marshals (Lamon and French?) are in the center, but most interesting is a seated Gov. Andrew Curtin with his son. (loc)

vast audience." Philip Bikle, a Pennsylvania College sophomore, occupied a choice spot directly in front of the speaker's stand. He recalled that Lincoln "spoke in a most deliberate manner, and with such forceful and articulate expression that he could be heard by all of that immense throng."

His delivery added much to the impressiveness of the speech. John Hay admitted that Lincoln, "in a firm, free way, with more grace than is his wont, said his half-dozen lines of consecration." Another account claimed, "We all noticed his earnestness and deep sincerity. He seemed to carry the nation's burden in his heart, and the audience became as earnest as he."

According to this account, Lincoln stood "as erect as one of his angularity could stand and rarely took his eyes from the paper. He swung backward and forward a little in speaking, as I have since seen Bismarck do, and he made no gestures." Bikle agreed, "There was no gesture except with both hands up and down, grasping the manuscript." William Tipton noted, "Lincoln used only one gesture during his entire speech, a wave of the hand when he came to that sentence: '—that these honored dead shall not have died in vain.'" Jacob Hoke recalled Lincoln's "closing words, which have become immortal, emphasizing each sentence with a brief pause and a significant nodding and jerking of his head."

Did Lincoln memorize his notes or read from them? Here again, the record is blurry. Some, like the account above, recalled Lincoln reading his notes, never looking up; others claimed he never looked down because he spoke the words from memory. Philip Bikle agreed, noting he grasped "the manuscript which he did not seem to need, as he looked at it seldom." It is hard to imagine Lincoln would have committed the entire speech to memory since he had not completed it until that very morning. However, as we will see below, the first page was written before Lincoln made the trip to Gettysburg,

This shot was probably taken at the conclusion of the ceremony. While the people on the left appear to be walking along the path to the platform, most of the others have turned and are walking away from it. (loc)

This photo shows soldiers, both mounted and on foot, at the consecration ceremony. Because of the location of Evergreen Gatehouse, these soldiers are not close to the platform but are awaiting the ceremony's conclusion so they can join the procession back to town. (loc)

providing him with plenty of time to memorize it. Historian Robert Bray additionally noted that Lincoln had a "near-flawless" memory. However, attorney general and Lincoln friend, James Speed, reported Lincoln later told him, that he "concluded it so shortly before it was to be delivered he had not time to memorize it."

How did the audience's respond? Applause is often a good gauge of the effectiveness of a speech and here (again) the record is contradictory. One observer recalled Lincoln "spoke slowly and was often interrupted by applause. To this he paid no attention, but when it subsided he read the next sentence, and so continued to the end, when a great storm of applause broke out." Calls for three cheers for Lincoln rang out, according to an observer, and then three more, this time for the governors. Others recalled not hearing any applause because the ceremony was "solemn." William Tipton noted, "the address was made before a crowd of mourners, many of whom had loved ones buried here or elsewhere" so it would have been inappropriate to clap "at the conclusion of a funeral oration." Some recalled the silence was bred by the brevity of the speech, which startled the audience. Gettysburg resident Alburtus McCreary may have summed it up best when he wrote, "I am sure he was listened to with greater attention, though only a few really understood the greatness of the words there and then spoken."

Several newspapers relied on the Associated Press for the transcriptions of the president's address, which included applause five times during

This stylized graphic shows Lincoln giving his immortal remarks. No officers occupied the first row, and Lincoln held a copy of his speech in one hand and may or may not have been reading it. Also not shown: Lincoln wearing his reading glasses. (loc)

the course of the remarks. John Young, a reporter for the *Philadelphia Press* sat on the platform during the ceremony and claimed long after the event, "I do not remember the applause, and am afraid the appreciative reporter was more than generous." He continued, "I have read of the tears that fell and the solemn hush, as though in a cathedral solemnity in the most holy moment of the sacrifice. There was nothing of this, to the writer at least, in the Gettysburg Address."

Like so many aspects of Lincoln's immortal speech, we are left with contradictory observations. However, if the Associated Press transcription, recorded in shorthand at the event is correct, then we are left with the belief that applause punctuated Lincoln's speech, especially at the end, when the reporter noted "long applause."

Time certainly influenced many a recollection. For example, Austin Bierbower recounted to a Chicago newspaper decades after the event, "Every sentence was felt and loudly applauded. I was strongly moved by it, thinking that it contained my sentiments as fully and exactly as if I had expressed them myself. He hit a great truth with every sentence or expressed deep feeling."

More telling were the comments of John Hay, Lincoln's secretary, who noted in his diary it "was Edward Everett's monumental oration which he did perfectly, as he always does" that carried the day. After that, Lincoln's few sentences seemed almost inadequate; or, at best, they came like the benediction, which you forget, after an impressive sermon, which you remember." College student Philip Bikle recalled, "On coming away I said to a classmate, 'Well, Mr. Lincoln's speech was . . . appropriate . . . but I don't think there was anything remarkable about it.'"

Historian William Barton summed the inconsistencies by positing, "there were as many different impressions as there were kinds of people in the audience." Barton believed most of the crowd had grown tired of standing through Everett's long oration and had pressed forward in anticipation as Lincoln rose to speak. His less-than-three-minute speech was over before they had a chance to settle in. The short speech was almost like no speech at all, so many were stunned when it ended so quickly, preventing a rousing round of applause of appreciation at the end, or high marks in general.

Gov. Tod selected Col. Charles Anderson to give the oration at the Ohio rally held at the Presbyterian Church. Severely wounded in battle, he later became governor of Ohio in 1865. (loc)

As Lincoln returned to his seat, he was met by Everett's and Curtin's warm words. Looking out upon the audience, Lincoln believed his speech had failed to move the audience. It was now time for the dirge, sung by a collection of singers accompanied by Birgfield's Band. The piece and its rendition were suitably morose for the occasion. As with the other musical numbers, it was given high marks.

Lamon next nodded to the final speaker and Rev. Henry Baugher, Gettysburg College's president, headed for center stage. "A semi-bald head, a hooked Roman nose, clear blue eye, and a decidedly clerical face. He would pass any where for a theological professor" was how a reporter described Baugher. His words of benediction were short and appropriate.

It was approximately 2:00 p.m. when Lamon informed the assemblage of the end of the program. He invited all to attend an Ohio-sponsored program to be held at 5:00 p.m. that night at the local Presbyterian Church on Baltimore Street. A battery from the 5th New York Artillery fired an eight-round salute as the marshals assembled the procession and shepherded it back up Baltimore Street. This column was shorter than the first as "many

The only known Gettysburg civilian who took up arms against the Confederates, John Burns was wounded three times, but used his experiences to gain fame and some fortune. It was only natural that Lincoln, thinking about his reelection campaign, would want to rub elbows with a national hero. (loc)

Although Gettysburg's Presbyterian Church began its work in 1740 operating out of a log structure three miles west of town, it built this church in 1842. The state of Ohio rented it for its political rally after the consecration ceremony. (gpc)

lingered until the shades of the evening approached, seemingly loath to leave the ground consecrated by the blood of those heroes who fought, died, and found a grave there."

Lincoln returned to the Wills house for a sumptuous dinner around 3:00 p.m. The president frequently sought opportunities to interact with citizens and after dinner was able to do just that. Wills stationed the president by his front door facing York Street. Those in the procession entered the door, shook hands with Lincoln, then continued through Wills's office to the side door, where they could grab Gov. Curtin's hand before exiting the home to the Square. Twelve-year-old Charles Young never forgot the scene, as "The line was passing rapidly with everybody bowing graciously to Lincoln." A newspaper explained that Lincoln was "subsequently visited by a large number of persons, and more than an hour was the victim of a 'hand shaking' that must have tested his good nature to the utmost."

Perhaps realizing the importance of the state of Ohio in the upcoming presidential election, Lincoln decided to attend a speech given by Col. Charles Anderson, a wounded war veteran and gifted speaker. Edward Everett recorded in his diary: "The poor president had to attend . . . I was too fatigued."

Lincoln was accompanied by Sec. Seward and the wizened 70-year-old Gettysburg resident John

Although the Presbyterian Church was torn down and rebuilt in 1963, an attempt was made to place a plaque on the approximate location of Lincoln's pew. (gpc)

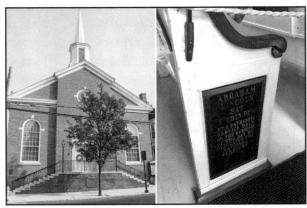

Burns. Burns was the only civilian known to have grabbed his firearm and ventured out to help fight the Rebels. Wounded three times, he was able to get home on Chambersburg Street while the battle blazed. Burns was not only an ornery cuss, he was also a Democrat. Some claimed he sat on the stage during the ceremony, but had not yet been introduced to the president. Upon meeting Burns, Lincoln is quoted as saying, "God bless you, old man" and the two walked arm in arm in the middle of Baltimore Street to the Presbyterian Church. Lincoln sat through yet another oration in the church filled to "repletion by an intelligent and highly respectable audience." While the *Ohio State Journal* reported Lincoln "expressed great satisfaction with Col. Anderson's effort," another paper noted that the exhausted president "bent his head on the back of the front set and quietly slept." Others claimed it was Burns who slept during the ceremony.

After the consecration ceremony, Lincoln greeted citizens at David Wills's house, standing at the front door on York Street. Then the line moved through Wills's house, and people shook hands with Gov. Andrew Curtin as they left the home through the side door on the right of the building. (loc)

Lincoln was not present when the program ended. His special train was leaving at 6:30 p.m. so he took his leave and walked back to the Wills house to thank his host and hostess for their hospitality and then headed to the train station. The trip was not a good one for Lincoln as he suffered from a severe headache, forcing him to lie down. The variola disease, a mild form of smallpox, may have been contracted from his son Tad was taking hold of his body. The disease would sicken him for several weeks, but he made a full recovery. The train finally reached Washington about midnight.

The town of Gettysburg had nearly cleared of its visitors by the end of the following day. The *Adams County Sentinel* perfectly captured what the townspeople already knew: it was a "perfect success." David Wills did not have time to savor his success—he immediately returned to his task as state agent and overseer of the burials at the National Soldiers Cemetery.

Writing the Gettysburg Address

CHAPTER TEN

November 3-18, 1863

Ask anyone where and when Lincoln wrote his Gettysburg Address and they might tell you, "on the back of an envelope while traveling to Gettysburg." This enduring fiction is now imprinted on the American psyche, even though it is patently false. The story came into being with Mary Shipman Andrews's small book entitled *The Perfect Tribute.* Apparently, Edward Everett provided information to Anson Burlingame, who related it to Walter Burlingame, who told Paul Andrews, who mentioned it to Mary Shipman Andrews. The story was embellished and changed along the way and is now etched in American culture. Mary Andrews intended her book to be fiction and took license, believing that all knew it was not an actual history of the event. According to historian Martin Johnson, the book was so "heartfelt . . . that it was incorporated into school texts across the nation."

Many principal players went out of their way to dispel the story, but it still remains. Let's begin with the train. Lincoln's personal secretary, John Nicolay, wrote that it could not have been written enroute to Gettysburg. He wrote, "The train consisted of four passenger coaches, and either composition or writing would have been extremely troublesome amid all the movement, the noise, the conversation, the greetings, and the questionings which ordinary courtesy required him to undergo

In Gettysburg's Diamond, a statue of Lincoln interacting with a statue of a modern tourist—collectively called "Return Visit"—invites visitors to look up at the room in the Wills house where Lincoln purportedly finished the Gettysburg Address. (cm)

John Nicolay and John G. Hay were friends from childhood, and in 1860 were selected to serve as Lincoln's personal secretary and assistant secretary. They served through his entire tenure as president and both went on to distinguished careers. (loc)

in these surroundings; but still worse would have been the rockings and joltings of the train, rendering writing virtually impossible."

The yellow envelope apparently arose from Gov. Andrew Curtin, who visited Lincoln on the evening of November 18 when he was still working on the address. He observed a "very large yellow envelope on which he was writing." The story morphed from Lincoln's room at the Wills house to the train. Over fifty years later, U. S. Congressman James Ashley claimed his saw Lincoln writing on a yellow envelope, using his top hat as a desk. Was there a yellow envelope? It appears that Everett had his oration printed and sent to the newspapers to ensure he was not misquoted during the ceremony. Lincoln received an advanced copy of Everett's speech on November 8, which helped him frame his own ideas without fear of seemingly usurping the main orator's ideas. At least one observer noted that Lincoln carried a yellow envelope with him to Gettysburg—possibly containing Everett's remarks and his own. Because of his exhaustive study of Lincoln's writings, Martin Johnson could write that Lincoln "would not have been averse to writing on an envelope if that was what was at hand at the moment . . . [he] wrote notes and thoughts on the back of unrelated documents and seemingly stray scraps of paper."

So, if Lincoln was not cavalier enough to compose his speech on a crowded train less than twenty-four hours prior to the ceremony and he did not use a scrap of paper, when and how did he write it? This is something of a mystery that has occupied probably thousands of hours of Lincoln's contemporaries and subsequent historians.

It now seems clear that Lincoln's Gettysburg address was not written in November, after he received his invitation. Some strongly posit that he had been writing these passages, at least in his head, almost as soon as the war began. They were born from a number of documents and ideas. The Declaration of Independence certainly was seminal, as was his strong support of the abolition of slavery. The long and gruesome war also influenced his thinking and the growing clamor of his opponents that it was now "Lincoln's war." Lincoln probably didn't need to think long and hard about what to say—he merely needed to commit it to paper in a way that could help his nation understand why the war was being waged and why the sacrifices were worth the horrendous losses.

"The Perfect Tribute" began as an article in *Scribner's Magazine* in 1906 but became a slim volume with sales of over 600,000. The story had a profound impact on the public's perception of Lincoln's Gettysburg Address because it was required reading for many schoolchildren. (lg)

One can look at Lincoln's speech on July 7 after the twin victories at Gettysburg and Vicksburg on July 4 to see some commonalities with his subsequent address: "How long is it?" Eighty-odd years, since upon the Fourth of July, for the first time in the world, a union body of representatives was assembled to declare as a self-evident truth that all men were created equal." It is clear that Lincoln built upon this idea, creating a more eloquent and compelling approach. According to historian Martin Johnson, the two speeches were the only times that Lincoln said what he believed deeply: all men are created equal."

But when did he pen the address? After his successful reelection bid, Lincoln sat down with old friend and Attorney General James Speed for a wide-ranging conversation. Lincoln admitted that his presidential responsibilities left but little time for him to craft what would become one of the

James Ashley was a distinguished Congressman representing a portion of Ohio. A leading Radical Republican, he pushed for the passage of the 13th Amendment. He later served as governor of Montana and the president of the Ann Arbor Railroad. (loc)

Abraham Lincoln appointed his good friend and fellow attorney James Speed to the post of U. S. attorney general in 1864, replacing Edward Bates. Prior to his appointment, he served in the Kentucky House of Representatives and worked diligently to keep the state in the Union. (loc)

most important speeches in world history. He had penned about half the speech, he recalled, before leaving for Gettysburg. This formed the first page of the draft, written in pen on Executive Mansion letterhead. The subsequent page used different paper and was written in pencil. After carefully considering the conflicting evidence, historian Martin Johnson believed that the first page was written on the evening of November 17, the day prior to his departure for Gettysburg. John Nicolay produced the document in Lincoln's bold hand with no changes until the end of the last sentence of that first page:

Four score and seven years ago our fathers brought forth on this continent, a new nation, conceived in Liberty, and dedicated to the proposition that all men are created equal.

Now we are engaged in a great civil war, testing whether that nation, or any nation so conceived, and so dedicated, can long endure. We are met on a great battle-field of that war. We have come to dedicate a portion of it, as a final resting place for those who died here, that the nation might live. This we may, in all propriety do. But, in a larger sense, we can not dedicate—we can not consecrate—we can not hallow—this ground. The brave men, living and dead, who struggled here, have hallowed it, far above our poor power to add or detract. The world will little note, nor long remember what we say here, while it can never forget what they did here. It is for us the living to stand here.

Lincoln headed for the train station with this page. Although he did not put pen to paper to complete his remarks during the journey, or earlier in the day when he had a full slate of meetings, it probably weighed heavily on his mind. He understood the importance of the event and the rare opportunity he would have to set the tone for the future of the nation.

Executive Mansion.

Washington,   186

Four score and seven years ago our fathers brought forth, upon this continent, a new nation, conceived in liberty, and dedicated to the proposition that "all men are created equal"

Now we are engaged in a great civil war, testing whether that nation, or any nation so conceived, and so dedicated, can long endure. We are met on a great battle field of that war. We have come to dedicate a portion of it, as a final resting place for those who died here that the nation might live. This we may, in all propriety do. But, in a larger sense, we can not dedicate — we can not consecrate — we can not hallow, this ground — The brave men, living and dead, who struggled here, have hallowed it, far above our poor power to add or detract. The world will little note, nor long remember what we say here; while it can never forget what they did here.

It is rather for us, the living, to stand here, [we here be] ted to the great task remaining before us — that, from these honored dead we take increased devotion to that cause for which they here, gave the last full measure of devotion — that we here highly resolve these dead shall not have died in vain; that the nation, shall have a new birth of freedom, and that government of the people by the people for, the people, shall not perish from the earth.

This is probably the copy of the Gettysburg Address Lincoln used during the Soldiers' Cemetery consecration. "Executive Mansion" can clearly be seen at the top of the first sheet, and the second sheet is clearly of a different type of stationery . (loc)

The timing of events becomes muddled as the years progress and this was true of Lincoln's return to his room at the Wills house after supper on the evening of November 18. Wills recalled it was "between nine and ten o'clock." As he put pencil to paper, Lincoln paused. He probably knew what he wanted to say, but were the words in keeping with what the Committee of Cemetery Commissioners intended? To ensure he was on the right track, Lincoln sent his groom, William Johnson, down to fetch Wills. Lincoln understood that 34-year-

Abraham Lincoln sat for this photograph a few weeks before he traveled to Gettysburg to give his famous address. (loc)

old Wills was the head of the committee that had invited him, so who better to get confirmation of his role. When Wills entered he "found him with paper prepared to write." According to Wills, "After a full talk on the subject I left him." It is possible that Lincoln may have shared some of his thoughts with Wills, for the latter wrote later, that he knew "all about" Lincoln's speech and "all he said to me about it." Satisfied that he was on the right track, Lincoln began crafting the remainder of his remarks. Legend has it that Lincoln borrowed paper and writing instruments from Wills, but the young attorney never confirmed it.

Lincoln's unexpected trip to visit Sec. Seward was undoubtedly to discuss his remarks. Although they were once rivals, the two had grown close, and Lincoln considered Seward to be one of his most trustworthy allies. He valued Seward's insights and hence the ambivalent president went to see his trusted advisor. Lincoln probably read his remarks to Seward who would have been expected to provide insights and perhaps some modifications.

We don't know what transpired between the two men at the Harper home. Sorting through conflicting information and muddled recollections, Martin Johnson surmised that when Lincoln visited Seward he carried with him his original first page written on Executive Mansion letterhead written in pen and a second page, crafted in pencil in his bedroom at the Wills's house. The short duration of the interactions suggests that Seward only suggested minor modifications.

Lincoln probably returned to his room, made some revisions to the remarks, and may have even copied them to a new piece of paper for clarity's sake. According to Martin Johnson, because Lincoln intended to take a tour of the battlefield of uncertain duration, "it simply would have been imprudent—hardly a Lincolnian trait—to have gone off on a tour of uncertain duration, with the unexpected possible complications . . . unless his text was in a state worthy of the grand day." The visit to the battlefield apparently had a profound impact on Lincoln, for when he returned to the Wills house, he again pulled out his remarks and modified them. The visit truly helped Lincoln get into the mood required to effectively consecrate the cemetery. For the first time, he may have put pencil to the pen strokes of the first page. John Nicolay recalled the fine tuning of Lincoln's speech took about an hour, so by 9:00 a.m. he was down at the Wills dining room having breakfast.

Lincoln was ready.

Which Gettysburg Address?

CHAPTER ELEVEN
November 19, 1863

The full-sized seated sculpture of Abraham Lincoln in front of the Gettysburg Visitors' Center captures the president as he may have appeared when he visited Gettysburg in 1863. It was sculpted by Ivan Schwartz and is a tourist favorite for snapping photos. The sculpture was dedicated on November 19, 2009—the 146th anniversary of the Gettysburg Address. (lg)

As Lincoln stepped to center stage on November 19 to utter his immortal words—words that millions around the world have committed to memory—the actual version of his remarks are unclear. In addition to the version on the paper Lincoln read, a reporter from the Associated Press used shorthand to record the speech and this was the one published in many newspapers. A year after the speech, Charles Hale claimed that he had transcribed the address and it was more accurate than the Associated Press version. In reality, only seven words separated the Associated Press version with Hale's transcription.

Why not simply accept Lincoln's script as the most accurate? Lincoln was known to stray from his written remarks so they were probably not the exact words he used during his address. One might think the version recorded by a competent stenographer would be the most accurate representation. Unfortunately, this is not the case as there were too many variables involved. Even if the stenographer had accurately captured every word, they had to be translated into Morse Code by the telegraph operator. Distortions in the line were not uncommon and upon receiving the transmission in New York City, another operator translated the Code back to English. Several minor errors might have occurred because of this process.

George Bancroft lived a life of service to the country. He served as secretary of war, founded the Naval Academy, served as U. S. minister to Prussia, and helped found the American Geographical Society. Like so many of the other copies of the Gettysburg Address, his copy was sold to a collector rather than benefit society. (loc)

Nevertheless, given the impressions of many who were present, it appears that the Associated Press version may be the most accurate representation of what Lincoln actually said:

Four score and seven years ago our fathers brought forth on this continent, a new nation, conceived in Liberty, and dedicated to the proposition that all men are created equal. [applause]

Now we are engaged in a great civil war, testing whether that nation, or any nation so conceived, and so dedicated, can long endure. We are met on a great battle-field of that war; we are met to dedicate a portion of it as the final resting place of those who here gave their lives that the nation might live. It is altogether fitting and proper that we should do this, but in a larger sense, we cannot dedicate, we cannot consecrate, we cannot hallow this ground.

The brave men, living and dead, who struggled here, have consecrated it far above our poor power to add or detract. [applause] *The world will little note, nor long remember what we say here, but it can never forget what they did here.* [applause] *It is for us, the living, rather to be dedicated here to the unfinished work that they have thus far so nobly carried on.* [applause] *It is rather for us here to be dedicated to the great task remaining before us; that from these honored dead we take increased devotion to that cause for which they here gave the last full measure of devotion; that we here highly resolve that these dead shall not have died in vain.* [applause] *That this nation shall, under God, have a new birth of freedom, and that government of the people, by the people, and for the people, shall not perish from the earth.* [long applause]

A careful analysis of Lincoln's written remarks and the Associated Press's version show minor differences in word choice that does not alter

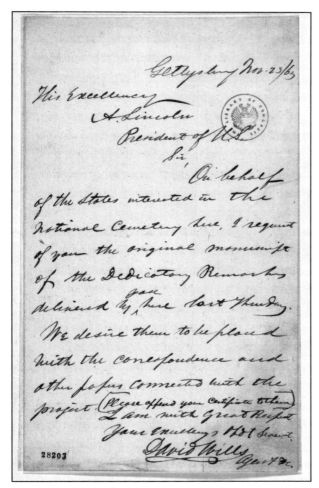

Many individuals requested a copy of Lincoln's remarks. David Wills asked to receive a copy "to be placed with the correspondence and other papers connected with the project." (loc)

the meaning of the passage. The most striking difference is Lincoln's inclusion of the words "under God" in the Associated Press version. Lincoln's trip to the battlefield that morning, the large crowd, and the mournful nature of the prior remarks and musical numbers probably added to Lincoln's sorrow and led him to add God to his speech. Mary Lincoln after the war noted that Lincoln became more spiritual as a result of the loss of his son and his trip to Gettysburg. She related that her husband was "not a technical Christian . . had no hope & no faith in the usual acceptance of those words: he never joined a church." Yet, "about the time he went to Gettysburg," Lincoln felt "religious—more than ever."

Lincoln may have made his first transcription of his remarks for Assistant Secretary John Hay. He had already begun the editing process by scribbling out some words and replacing them with others. (loc)

Historians have also debated which version of the Gettysburg Address Lincoln read from on November 19. Lincoln prepared at least five different copies of his address and each one is a bit different from the others. Most historians now agree that Lincoln used the **Nicolay copy** for his speech. The first page is written in pen on "Executive Mansion" stationery; the second in pencil on foolscap paper. Lincoln gave his senior secretary this version and it now is housed at the Library of Congress.

Lincoln wrote at least four other copies after he returned to Washington:

The **Hay copy** is probably the first replica in Lincoln's hand. It differs somewhat from the original primarily in punctuation and word choices. Like the subsequent copies, this version differed from the original in being written entirely in ink. Like the Nicolay copy, it does not add the words, "under God." This version is also owned by the Library of Congress.

> Four score and seven years ago our fathers brought forth upon this continent, a new nation, conceived in Liberty, and dedication to the proposition that all men are created equal,
>
> Now we are engaged in a great civil war, testing whether that nation, or any nation so conceived, and so dedicated, can long endure. We are met on a great battle field of that war. We have come to dedicate a portion of that field, as a final resting place for those who here gave their lives, that that nation might live. It is altogether fitting and proper that we should do this.
>
> But, in a larger sense, we can not dedicate— we can not consecrate— we can not hallow— this ground. The brave men, living and dead, who struggled here, have consecrated it, far above our poor power to add or detract. The world will little note, nor long remember, what we say here, but it can never forget what they did here. It is for us, the living, rather, to be dedicated here to the unfinished work which they who fought here, have, thus far, so nobly advanced. It is rather for us to be here dedicated to the great task remaining before
>
> us— that from these honored dead we take increased devotion to that cause for which they here gave the last full measure of devotion— that we here highly resolve that these dead shall not have died in vain— that this nation, under God, shall have a new birth of freedom— and that, government of the people, by the people, for the people, shall not perish from the earth.

Lincoln's third copy of his address went to Edward Everett. He retained some of the changes made in Hays's copy, but not others. Lincoln made no scratch-outs on this document, probably because it was to be sold for the war effort. It was the first copy to contain the words "under God." (loc)

The U.S. Sanitary Commission, the precursor of the American Red Cross, organized fairs throughout the country to raise money for its critically important mission. Wanting to support this effort, **Edward Everett** asked Lincoln for a copy of his address that could be sold at the New York's Sanitary Commission Fair in April 1864. A copy of the Emancipation Proclamation had sold at the Chicago Fair for the large sum (back then) of $3,000, so Everett thought the address could fetch at least that amount. Lincoln obliged, making it the third copy of the speech. With this copy, Lincoln began adding the phrase, "under God," which he apparently included in his remarks at Gettysburg. This copy was never sold as planned, but eventually found its way into the hands of a

The first page of Lincoln's fourth copy is similar to Everett's copy, except he did not include some of the punctuation marks at the bottom of the first page. It is the only copy in private hands. (loc)

wealthy Boston merchant. It was later sold to the Illinois State Historical Library and now resides at the Lincoln's Presidential Library and Museum on Springfield, Illinois.

A fourth copy went to historian **George Bancroft**, former Secretary of the Navy and eminent historian. Like Everett, Bancroft wished to prepare a publication to be sold at a Sanitary Fair—this one in Baltimore. The publication would be entitled, Autograph Leaves of Our Country's Authors and Bancroft approached Lincoln, who prepared the transcription in February 1864. Unfortunately, Lincoln wrote his address on both sides of one sheet of paper, making it unusable during the lithographic process. Bancroft retained this copy and later sold it to a collector. It was later donated to Cornell University. It is the only privately owned copy.

When told his draft could not be used for reproduction, Lincoln sat down and prepared

Address delivered at the dedication of the Cemetery at Gettysburg.

Four score and seven years ago our fathers brought forth on this continent, a new nation, conceived in Liberty, and dedicated to the proposition that all men are created equal.

Now we are engaged in a great civil war, testing whether that nation, or any nation so conceived and so dedicated, can long endure. We are met on a great battle-field of that war. We have come to dedicate a portion of that field, as a final resting place for those who here gave their lives that that nation might live. It is altogether fitting and proper that we should do this.

But, in a larger sense, we can not dedicate—we can not consecrate—we can not hallow—this ground. The brave men, living and dead, who struggled here, have consecrated it, far above our poor power to add or detract. The world will little note, nor long remember what we say here, but it can never forget what they did here. It is for us the living, rather, to be dedicated here to the unfinished work which they who fought here have thus far so nobly advanced. It is rather for us to be here dedicated to the great task remaining before us—that from these honored dead we take increased devotion to that cause for which they gave the last full measure of devotion—that we here highly resolve that these dead shall not have died in vain—that this nation, under God, shall have a new birth of freedom—and that government of the people, by the people, for the people, shall not perish from the earth.

Abraham Lincoln.

November 19, 1863.

a fifth draft. This eventually went to **Col. Alexander Bliss**, George Bancroft's stepson. It is the only copy signed and dated by Lincoln. The Bliss family eventually sold the document and it was ultimately purchased by Oscar Cintas, the Cuban Ambassador to the United States in 1949. He willed it to the American people with the provision that it be kept at the White House, where it now hangs on the wall of the Lincoln bedroom. It is of interest to note that it is this, the last copy that Lincoln transcribed, that is most commonly referred to as "Lincoln's Gettysburg Address."

Lincoln signed and dated the last copy of his address. This copy is in the White House. (loc)

David Wills will continue to reside in Gettysburg until his death in 1894 at the age of 63, actively serving Adams County and the Borough of Gettysburg. (loc)

Reactions to the Gettysburg Address

CHAPTER TWELVE

November 19, 1863-April 19, 1865

As we saw in Chapter 10, at the time of the ceremony there was a variety of reactions to Lincoln's short address. Through time, the public's perceptions of the speech changed radically as it earned universal acclaim. This was certainly not the case in the days following the consecration ceremony. Even Lincoln's trusted secretary, John Hay, noted in his diary that it "was Edward Everett's monumental oration which he did perfectly, as he always does" that carried the day. After that, Lincoln's few sentences seemed almost inadequate; or, at best, they came like the benediction, which you forget, after an impressive sermon, which you remember."

Newspapers have always been a gauge of public perceptions, but here the reception of Lincoln's remarks came down to politics: Republican papers loved it; their Democratic counterparts hated it. One needs only to glance at the Illinois newspapers to see how this played out. *The Chicago Times* accused Lincoln of "ignorant rudeness," boorishness," and "vulgarity," for including "political partisanship" in his address. It called Lincoln's remarks, "silly, flat and dishwatery." The paper was especially upset with his statement that "all men are created equal." Lincoln's Democratic-leaning hometown paper, the *Illinois State Register*, also took up the *Times's* refrain: "he uttered the words he knew he was falsifying

The Soldiers' National Monument is located at the center of the National Cemetery and features five seated figures sitting on buttresses and a large figure at the top representing the concept of Liberty. The cornerstone was laid on July 4, 1965, and the monument was completed in 1869. (cm)

We pass over the silly remarks of the President. For the credit of the nation we are willing that the veil of oblivion shall be dropped over them, and that they shall be no more repeated or thought of.

Harrisburg's *Patriot & Union*, a democratic newspaper, denigrated Lincoln's speech in its November 24, 1863, edition, calling his remarks "silly" and willing to drop the "veil of oblivion" over them. The newspaper's successor, the *Patriot-News*, printed a retraction almost 150 years later. (pl)

history, and enunciating an exploded political humbug." The Republican papers took the opposite tack. The *Illinois State Journal* wrote that Lincoln's speech generated "immense applause, and three cheers given for him, and also three cheers for the governors of the states." The Republican-leaning *Chicago Tribune* concentrated on Everett's oration, calling it, "the best style and vein of the 'model orator,' and will well repay perusal," but predicted that it was Lincoln's remarks that "will live among the annals of man."

Other newspapers were equally mixed, again, depending on their political leanings. The *Philadelphia Public Ledger* wrote that "the short, modest, fitting address of the President of the United States produced tears at times, and at times every other emotion as only the highest eloquence can." It was counterbalanced by the *Harrisburg Patriot News*, which noted the "silly remarks of the President" and said: "for the credit of the nation we are willing that the veil of oblivion shall be dropped over them [Lincoln's remarks] and that they shall be no more repeated or thought of."

How did Lincoln view his speech? If one believes Ward Lamon, not well. On his return to Washington, Lamon recalled Lincoln telling him "that speech fell on the audience like a wet blanket. I am distressed about it. I ought to have prepared it with more care." Wayne McVeagh approached Lincoln after the ceremony, commenting "with great earnestness, "You have made an immortal address." Lincoln responded, "Oh, you must not say that. You must not be extravagant about it." McVeagh called this "inexplicable."

In reality, we don't really know how Lincoln viewed his speech immediately after the ceremony. He may not have given it much thought as he was beginning to feel the effects of variola, which would lay him low for several weeks. Lincoln received reinforcement from an important source immediately after returning to Washington. Although Everett did not mention Lincoln's address in his diary, he wrote to him the day after the ceremony expressing thanks for the kindness shown to his daughter. He added his "great admiration" for the "eloquent simplicity & appropriateness" of his remarks. Everett also told Lincoln, "I should be glad, if I could flatter myself that I came as near to the central idea of the occasion, in two hours, as you did in two minutes." Such comments from an orator as distinguished as Everett elevated Lincoln. He immediately sat down and penned a response: "I am pleased to know that in your judgment, the little I did say was not entirely a failure." He also took the opportunity to compliment Everett on his "eminently satisfactory" oration. Lincoln later told his attorney general, James Speed, that "he had never received a compliment he prized more highly" than the one he received from Everett.

Henry Wadsworth Longfellow was a literary lion and one of the greatest poets of his time. Sparse in his praise, his opinion of Lincoln's speech carried much weight. (loc)

Henry Wadsworth Longfellow, who had eschewed the invitation to pen an ode for the ceremony, read about Lincoln's speech in a newspaper and told his friend, George Curtis, that it "seemed admirable." Curtis, a distinguished author in his own right, and political editor of *Harper's Weekly*, scrutinized Lincoln's address and wrote early in 1864, "The few words of the President were from the heart to heart." He added "They cannot be read, even, without kindling emotion. 'The world will little note nor long remember what we say, but it can never forget what they did here.' It was as simple and felicitous and earnest a word as was ever spoken," he noted in a December issue of the *Harper's Weekly*. This was followed in the April issue with an editorial calling Lincoln's speech "the most perfect piece of American eloquence." A large number of scholars also scrutinized Lincoln's

British historian, journalist, and educator Goldwin Smith was well known and respected on both sides of the "pond." His support for the North was strong, and he was vocal about it. (loc)

remarks during his lifetime and found them worthy of praise. For example, Oxford University professor Goldwin Smith wrote in *Macmillan's Magazine* that Lincoln was "the greatest orator of the United States," and printed the Gettysburg Address to show why. On this side of the pond, eminent poet Ralph Waldo Emerson noted in 1865 that Lincoln's "brief speech at Gettysburg will not easily be surpassed by words on any recorded occasion." These are but two examples of the profound impact of Lincoln's words within a year and a half after the ceremony. The praise of other distinguished writers and leaders added during Lincoln's soon-to-end lifetime, probably caused him to feel very positively about his speech and its impact.

The movement to sanctify the Gettysburg Address as one of the greatest speeches in American history gained steam in the 1880s as a flood of "recollections" was printed in books, articles, and newspapers. Lincoln's good friend and marshal of the ceremony, Ward Lamon, would have nothing of it, as he hated the "falsification of history." He was particularly bothered by Lincoln being valued "not as a human being endowed with a mighty intellect and extraordinary virtues, but as a god." Lamon wrote that he viewed the speech positively from the start for its "marvelous perfection, the intrinsic excellence of the Gettysburg speech as a masterpiece of English composition," but lamented that at the time it "seems to have escaped the scrutiny of even the most scholarly critics of the day." As seen above, this was simply untrue.

As the 20th century dawned, Lincoln's Gettysburg address had taken its place as perhaps the most valued speech in United States history. Hundreds of accounts of the speech published long after it was uttered spoke only positively about it. By 1913 the *Philadelphia Evening Bulletin* could write, "Perhaps only the Lord's Prayer exceeds it [Lincoln's Gettysburg Address] as a familiar composition to American minds." Generations of school children were made to memorize and recite the Gettysburg Address, further cementing it in

Americans' psyche. The reverence for the speech spread to other countries and they too required students to memorize the speech's passages. In the United States, the Address became center stage during national tragedies, such as the terrorist attacks on 9/11 and the attack on Pearl Harbor.

So strong was the push to immortalize the speech that on its 150th anniversary, the Harrisburg *Patriot-News* symbolically retracted its original coverage, which called Lincoln's remarks, "silly." The *Patriot-News's* opinion editor, John Micek, explained the rationale: "Our panning of the Gettysburg Address has long been a part of the *Patriot-News* lore and always a bit of a nettle in our side, given our proximity to Gettysburg [about 30 miles away] and the huge place the battle has in the region's history. With the 150th anniversary of the address on Tuesday, the time seemed right to correct the record."

The Gettysburg Address' Meaning and Enduring Legacy of Gettysburg

CHAPTER THIRTEEN

November 19, 1863

Historians have teased four themes in the speech: A harkening back to the country's founding in which "all men are created equal," explicitly recognizing the sacrifices of the country's soldiers, particularly those who perished fighting for liberty, explaining that only the dead could hallow and consecrate the cemetery, and providing a message of hope for the future.

> *Four score and seven years ago our fathers brought forth on this continent, a new nation, conceived in Liberty, and dedicated to the proposition that all men are created equal.*

Lincoln was profoundly influenced by the Declaration of Independence and he once said, "I have never had a feeling politically that did not spring from the sentiments embodied" in that document. Earlier in the war, Lincoln kept his strong feelings about the Declaration of Independence and its unique phrase that "all men are created equal," in check lest he antagonize the Border States and antagonize Northerners.

> *Now we are engaged in a great civil war, testing whether that nation, or any nation so conceived, and so dedicated, can long endure.*

Dedicated in 1975, "Kentucky honors her son" bears the Bluegrass State's seal and reproduces the Gettysburg Address. It sits in the national cemetery near the base of the soldiers' monument. (cm)

Laying the monument's cornerstone, July 4, 1864. (loc)

In this single sentence, Lincoln asks whether the uncommon experiment of democracy can survive internal strife that threatened to tear it apart. Other nations governed by monarchs or despots, watched with interest, hoping the democratic movement would die with the United States.

We are met on a great battle-field of that war; we are met to dedicate a portion of it as the final resting place of those who here gave their lives that the nation might live. It is altogether fitting and proper that we should do this, but in a larger sense, we cannot dedicate, we cannot consecrate, we cannot hallow this ground.

The brave men, living and dead, who struggled here, have consecrated it far above our poor power to add or detract. The world will little note, nor long remember what we say here, but it can never forget what they did here.

Here Lincoln gets to the meat of the consecration ceremony. In beautifully crafted statements, he recognizes the men's sacrifices. The living, he writes, cannot consecrate the cemetery—only the dead could do that through their valiant deeds.

It is for us, the living, rather to be dedicated here to the unfinished work that they have thus far so nobly carried on. It is rather for us here to be dedicated to the great task remaining before us; that from these honored dead we take increased devotion to that cause for which they here gave the last full measure of devotion; that we here highly resolve that these dead shall not have died in vain. That this nation shall, under God, have a new birth of freedom, and that government of the people, by the people, and for the people, shall not perish from the earth.

The final section is a call to action to continue the fight. It is only through the continuation of the fight that the men being buried here would not have died in vain. The successful conclusion

Order of Exercises in the Cemetery.

Music—Band.

PRAYER BY THE REV. STEPHEN H. TYNG, D. D.

Music—"French's Hymn"—Union Musical Association.

INTRODUCTORY REMARKS BY THE PRESIDENT OF THE UNITED STATES.

Music—"Hayward's Ode"—Union Musical Association.

LAYING OF THE CORNER STONE BY THE GRAND MASTER OF THE GRAND LODGE OF MASONS OF PENNSYLVANIA.

ADDRESS BY THE GOVERNOR OF PENNSYLVANIA.

Music—Band.

ORATION BY MAJOR GENERAL O. O. HOWARD.

Music—Band.

POEM BY COL. C. G. HALPINE.

Music—Union Musical Association.

BENEDICTION—By Rev. D. T. CARNAHAN.

Music—Band.

The cornerstone of the monument in the Soldiers' Cemetery was laid on July 4, 1865, to another large gathering. The program was much shorter than the one during the consecration ceremony less than two years before. (loc)

The still-to-be-finished Soldiers' Monument was dedicated on July 1, 1869. Gen. George Meade was one of the keynote speakers. (hw)

of the fight would lead to a new birth of freedom as the very heart of democracy is sustained.

No American battlefield generates as much enthusiasm as Gettysburg. It has all the elements needed for a special place in our history. It was the largest battle on American soil, generating the greatest number of casualties. It also changed the face of the war, as Robert E. Lee could no longer mount a large offensive campaign. The development and consecration of the cemetery was unique. Nowhere else was a cemetery formed by the general public so soon after the conclusion of the battle and it was the only one that counted Abraham Lincoln as a speaker. There were many reasons for Lincoln to skip the visit to Gettysburg, but he was drawn by the opportunity to explain why the sacrifices made by families needed to continue. The nation could not be ripped apart by fundamental differences that revolved primarily around slavery. The war had come down to a struggle for the very heart and soul of the nation.

There were many heroes associated with Gettysburg, beginning of course, with those who made the ultimate sacrifice. The leadership of Gettysburg citizens, such as David Wills and David McConaughy, illustrate what Americans can do in a crisis, and of course, Abraham Lincoln who steadfastly worked to cement our nation together. The story of Gettysburg is not merely the battle, or Lincoln's speech, it is the totality of the events that illustrate the American spirit and as such, it will always occupy a special place in our legacy.

> The Soldiers' National Monument at Gettysburg.
>
> GETTYSBURG, Penn., Sunday, May 30.
>
> All the military organizations of the country are invited to participate in the ceremonies of the dedication of the monument in the Soldiers' National Cemetery at Gettysburg, on the 1st of July next, and those intending to be present are requested to communicate such intentions within a reasonable time, so that proper arrangements may be made for them. The call is signed by DAVID WELLS, Chairman.

The notice of the July 1, 1869, dedication of the Soldiers' Monument was published in *The New York Times* on May 31, 1869. Note that David Wills's name is spelled incorrectly. (nyt)

A Tour of Lincoln's Activities at Gettysburg

APPENDIX A

Although Abraham Lincoln's visit to Gettysburg lasted about 25 hours, he visited, or was in contact with, a variety of now-historic sites. This tour takes you to most of them.

Stop 1 – Train Station

35 Carlisle Street

Begin your tour at the Gettysburg Train Station. Passenger and freight service officially began on December 17, 1858, and it had a tremendous impact on commerce and travel. You will see two doors opening onto Carlisle Street. During the time of Lincoln's visit, the small waiting room was subdivided by a wall. The men's section on the right contained spittoons and the ticket counter. The left room was for women and children. If you are able to enter the train station, you will see the dividing wall is gone, but the doors remain.

During the battle, the train station was used as a hospital, and some of the wounded were able to climb the steps to the cupola and watch the battle. Their graffiti on the walls of the cupola remains to this day.

Lincoln's train arrived between 6:00 and 6:30 p.m. Historians believe he walked through the train station, exiting through the men's side of the waiting room. He was quickly engulfed by a sea of visitors who arrived to watch the "once-in-a-lifetime event." Many heard of Lincoln's arrival and made their way to the station, but were disappointed when they were unable to see him because of the large crowd.

The sign outside the Taneytown Road entrance to the National Cemetery beckons visitors by the thousands every year. Parking considerations cause this entrance to be the one of choice by most visitors. (lg)

If Lincoln looked across the street, he would have seen the Washington Hotel, a popular lodging spot for visitors to the town. It too was a hospital during the battle and was hit by as many as two shells. It was later used as an embalming studio after the battle. Its proximity to the train station was ideal. The embalmers plied their trade, placed the corpse in a coffin, and sent it across the street to be placed on a train, where it could be taken to any part of the North.

Stop 2 – The Square (Diamond)

Walk up Carlisle Street toward the Square. You are following in Lincoln's footsteps to what local citizens called the "Diamond." The Diamond was the center of activity during the time of Lincoln's visit. Graced with a tall flagpole, it stood witness to the activities that transpired during this period.

When entering and exiting the train station, women used the left door and men the right. The right side contained a number of spittoons and the ticket window. Lincoln probably exited through the right door to reach Carlisle Street. (lg)

Before we continue down Baltimore Street, look down Carlisle, Chambersburg, and York Streets. During the run-up to the consecration ceremony, the various groups assembled in theses streets and then came together to form the procession heading down Baltimore Street to the cemetery.

Stop 3 – Wills House

8 Lincoln Square

The Wills house was totally renovated in 2009 and returned to its original splendor. Lincoln's bedroom, which measures 14 feet wide by 22 feet long with nine-foot ceilings, is the centerpiece of the home. (lg)

We don't know much about Lincoln's walk to reach the David Wills house. Artists have represented him walking in the center of Carlisle Street accompanied by those who traveled with him to Gettysburg. The house is on York Street.

Once in the house, Lincoln was shown to his room on the second floor where he rested and freshened up prior to dinner. His room was the third window from the right (facing the square). The iconic sculpture on the sidewalk outside by J. Seward Johnson, placed in 1991, shows Lincoln pointing to his room as a visitor holds a copy of the Gettysburg Address. Because Johnson used life masks of Lincoln's face and hands, and drawings of his boots and suit, it is considered one of the most accurate representations of Lincoln.

The Wills House has two doors—the main door on York Street and the entrance to David Wills's law office on the Square. Lincoln most likely used the main entrance when he gave a short speech on the evening of November 18, and to enter and leave the building on November 19. After the consecration cemetery, Lincoln wished to greet his many admirers. He positioned himself at Wills's front door and

Publisher Robert Harper owned a home that matched his wealth and reputation. Located next to David Wills's home (a portion of it is on the left of the photo) on the Diamond, it played host to a number of influential guests, including Sec. of State William Seward. The building in this photo sits on the original home's footprint. (lg)

welcomed the guests as they arrived. They next walked through the home, through Wills's law office and exited through the door on the Square. As they did, they shook hands with Pennsylvania Governor Andrew Curtin. The National Park Service and Gettysburg Foundation jointly administer the property and charge an entry fee.

This view of Baltimore Street from the Square was taken after the Civil War. The procession for the Soldiers' National Cemetery's dedication assembled on the three streets entering the square and then marched down Baltimore Street. (achs)

Stop 4 – Robert Harper Home

10 Lincoln Square

This modern view of Baltimore Street is looking north toward the Square. Union sharpshooters were able to hit soldiers as far as the rise up ahead. (lg)

Directly next door (and attached) to the Wills House on the Square was the home of Robert Harper, publisher and owner of the Adams Sentinel, a Republican-leaning newspaper. Several dignitaries lodged here on the evening of November 18-19. When Lincoln completed his draft of the Gettysburg Address during the evening of November 18, Lincoln exited David Wills's law office door and walked a short distance to the entrance of Harper's home. Secretary of State William Seward was lodging there, and Lincoln wanted him to see his remarks. The crush of humanity was so great Lincoln held onto the coattails of his guard as the two navigated from the Wills house to Harper's home.

Stop 5—Baltimore Street

Walk down Baltimore Street and imagine you are part of this massive column slowly making its way to the cemetery. The military, with fixed bayonets, led the procession, followed by elected officials/dignities, and ordinary folks brought up the rear. Homes present during the Civil War are marked by a bronze rectangular plate by their front doors. These were put in place during the battle's centennial.

Stop 6—Statue of Lincoln in front of the Gettysburg Library

140 Baltimore Street

The imposing statue of Abraham Lincoln was placed in front of the library in 2013 as part of the Remembrance Day events during the battle's sesquicentennial. The eight-foot statue depicts Lincoln delivering his Gettysburg Address. It was crafted by Utah artist Stanley J. Watts. It is an interesting contrast to Johnson's sculpture on the Square.

No one knows for sure if Lincoln held a copy of his Gettysburg address or used grand hand gestures. This is one of the more dramatic representations of Lincoln in and around Gettysburg. (lg)

Stop 7—Presbyterian Church

208 Baltimore Street

The Presbyterian Church you see on your left has changed dramatically from its appearance in 1863. The congregation dates back to 1740 when it began hosting services in a log structure three miles west of town. The church occupied this location since 1842, and its current building dates from 1963. It contains the original rafters and is the same dimension of the 1863

The Presbyterian Church was the only one of Gettysburg's houses of worship that played a role during Lincoln's visit to Gettysburg. Check out the multiple plaques on the front of the building, which also served as a hospital during the battle. (lg)

building. All of the pews were replaced, except for Lincoln's. The president attended the political rally hosted by the State of Ohio after the cemetery's consecration. Local hero John Burns, the only civilian who picked up arms and fought against the Confederates during the battle, was by his side. President Dwight D. Eisenhower and his wife, Mamie, became members of the church in 1963 and like Lincoln's, their pew is designated.

The first 50-star flag is displayed in the church's foyer. It was presented to President Eisenhower after he signed the proclamation making Hawaii our 50th state in 1959. The flag was first displayed in the Oval office and then was presented to the church in 1960.

Stop 8 – Witness Tree

404 Baltimore Street

Continue walking down Baltimore Street until you come to Lefever Street. Here you can see the two "witness trees" that watched the procession moving slowly toward the cemetery. One of the trees is in front of 404 Baltimore Street; the other across Lefever Street.

These two sycamore trees are the most conspicuous witness trees in and around Gettysburg. The one to the north sat in front of the John Winebrenner home, which is now a commercial store. The one closest to Cemetery Hill was near the Samuel McCreary home. The latter was torn down to accommodate a broader entrance to the schools behind it. (lg)

Unity Park is across Lefever Street. It was the brainchild of 14-year old Andrew Adam, a central-Pennsylvania student completing his Eagle Scout requirements. The park features a statue of a Union drummer boy, which was near and dear to Andrew, as he performed this role in a reenactor unit. The 36 bushes represent the number of states in the Union at the end of the war. One walkway represents the North, another the South and the one in the center represents "Unity."

This was an area of fighting on July 2 and 3 as sharpshooters of both sides plied their trade. The south-facing side of "Mr. G's" Ice Cream Parlor and the "Farnsworth House" across the street bore witness to the fighting that occurred here.

You may wish to continue walking down Baltimore Street to the National Cemetery.

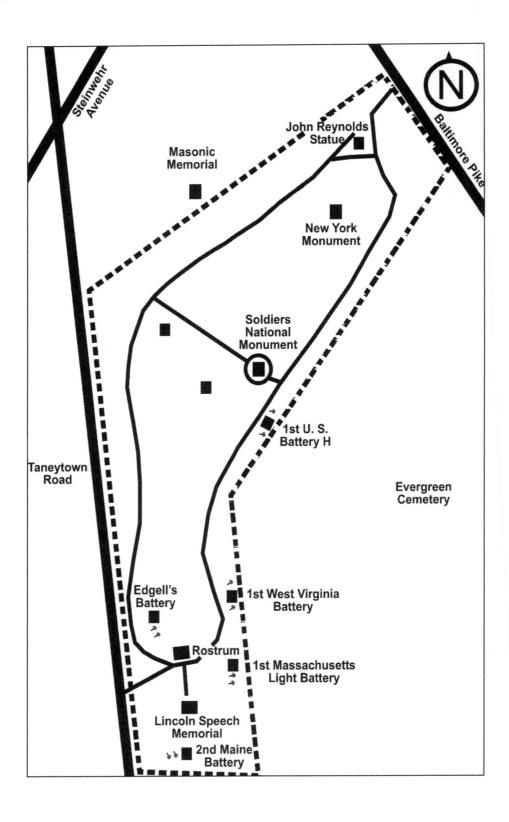

A Tour of the National Cemetery

APPENDIX B

A wonderful way to experience any period in history is to walk the same ground once tread upon by our predecessors. The journey opens our eyes and imaginations in ways just reading cannot unlock. Below is a guide to touring the Soldiers' National Cemetery. You can follow in its entirety or in parts. We encourage you to walk in the footsteps of Lincoln and his contemporaries – it is our hope you will understand and appreciate the history of Gettysburg in a whole new way.

The Soldiers' Cemetery was established in 1863 to bury Union soldiers who died at Gettysburg. The cemetery contains more than 3,500 graves from that battle. Other veterans were added to the cemetery—3,307 of them—before it closed for further burials of veterans in 1972. Although there are 141 National Cemeteries in 40 states, the Pennsylvania-owned Gettysburg Soldiers' Cemetery was ceded to the Federal Government in 1872 and is one of only 14 administered by the United States National Park Service. As you enter the cemetery, please be aware it is sacred ground. Noise should be kept to a minimum and eating and drinking are prohibited.

We recommend you enter the cemetery through the Taneytown Road entrance. You will find parking in the lot across the street. There are 13 stops on this tour; it roughly follows the National Park Service Tour route.

Stop 1 – Cemetery Entrance

As you enter the cemetery, you will see three memorials. The **Rostrum** to your left was built in 1879 and is used for special ceremonies, such as the Remembrance Day speech, which is presented by a dignitary each year. In addition, at least six presidents have used it for Memorial Day ceremonies: Rutherford B. Hayes, Theodore Roosevelt, Calvin Coolidge, Herbert Hoover, Franklin D. Roosevelt, and Dwight D. Eisenhower (also,

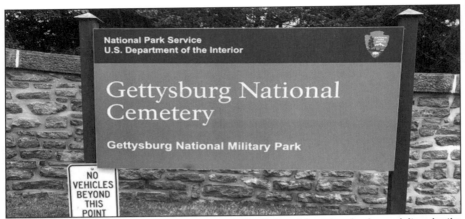

The sign outside the Taneytown Road entrance to the National Cemetery beckons visitors by the thousands every year. Parking considerations cause this entrance to be the one of choice by most visitors. (lg)

Lyndon B. Johnson who was vice-president at the time of his speech, but later became president). Interesting side note: President John F. Kennedy was scheduled to speak at the Remembrance Day Ceremony in November 1963, but opted to travel to Dallas where he was assassinated on November 22, 1963.

To your right is the **Lincoln Speech Memorial**. Erected in 1912, it commemorates Lincoln's extraordinary Gettysburg Address. Very few memorials in the world are dedicated to a single speech. Sculptor Henry Bush-Brown created the bust of Lincoln. If you look carefully you will see the effect of the war on Lincoln's countenance. David Wills's letter inviting Lincoln to speak at the cemetery's consecration ceremony is to Lincoln's left. It reads in part, "It is the desire that you as Chief Executive of the Nation formally set apart these grounds to their sacred use by a few appropriate remarks." Lincoln's Gettysburg Address is to the right of the bust.

A monument to the **2nd Maine Battery** is nearby. The six-gun battery was commanded by Capt. James Hall during the battle. This battery was composed of six, three-inch ordnance rifles that could throw a shell over a mile. If you place your hand inside the barrel you will feel the groves which propelled shells with great speed and accuracy. This battery was among the first to be put into service on the morning of July 1. Their position near Chambersburg Pike was overwhelmed by the counterattack by Brig. Gen. Joseph Davis's Brigade and barely escaped. Hall's battery eventually fell back to this position, where it shelled Confederate artillery on July 2. The battery was so devastated during the first day's fight it was ordered to the rear on July 3 to refit. The primary monument to the 2nd Maine Battery sits on Chambersburg Pike, across the road from the West End Guide Station.

Stop 2 – 1st Massachusetts Light Battery Monument

Return to the main path and continuing walking. You will see the section of the cemetery dedicated to the Gettysburg dead on your left. Stop at the monument to the 1st Massachusetts Battery on the right of the path. This is another of several monuments marking the position of Union artillery on the second and third days of the battle. The hill rumbled with more than 70 Union cannon raining death and destruction on Confederate artillery positions and troop formations to the north of Gettysburg (to your left) and along Seminary Ridge to the west (behind you).

The 1st Massachusetts Light Battery was commanded by Captain William H. McCartney during the battle of Gettysburg. The battery arrived on Cemetery Hill at 4:00 p.m. on July 3, too late to help repulse the Pickett-Pettigrew-Trimble Charge. As a result, it only fired four rounds during the battle.(lg)

Stop 3 – 1st West Virginia (Huntington's) Battery

This battery was commanded by Wallace Hill during the battle. Its four, 10-pounder Parrotts have a characteristic reinforcing band around the breech end of each barrel preventing the gun from exploding. These cannon could shoot a projectile over 2,000 yards. The left and right flank markers behind the guns give a good indication of the position the battery occupied during the battle.

As you walk from Stop 2 to Stop 3, you will see these small flank markers. This is the position of the left cannon of Battery H, 1st Ohio Light Artillery. There is a corresponding stone for the battery's right cannon. These stones are examples of John Bachelder's work with veterans after the war to designate the actual position of most Union units on the battlefield. (lg)

Stop 4 – Poems, Fences, and Trees

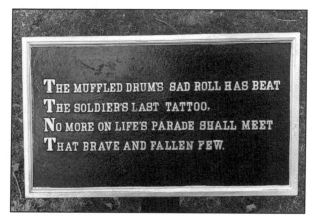

THE MUFFLED DRUM'S SAD ROLL HAS BEAT
THE SOLDIER'S LAST TATTOO,
NO MORE ON LIFE'S PARADE SHALL MEET
THAT BRAVE AND FALLEN FEW.

Kentuckian Theodore O'Hara, who wrote the poem "Bivouac of the Dead," was a quartermaster captain during the War with Mexico. After leaving the army, he resumed his Washington, D.C., law practice and then turned to journalism. He was an officer in the Confederate army during the Civil War and died in 1874. (lg)

Stop at the marker with a poem on your left. This is the opening stanza of a poem entitled, "Bivouac of the Dead," written by Theodore O'Hara to honor Americans slain at the Battle of Buena Vista (1847) during the Mexican War. Discover other stanzas of the poem as you walk through the cemetery.

Look to your right. You will see the fence separating the National Cemetery from the local Evergreen Cemetery. Shortly after the battle, another skirmish raged between David Wills, who wanted to establish a separate cemetery for the Gettysburg dead, and David McConaughy, who argued for the location to be within the existing Evergreen Cemetery. Wills ultimately won this battle, but it was an ugly fight. McConaughy purchased the land for what is now the National Cemetery and finally agreed to sell it to the state at his own cost. The two sides agreed a simple metal fence would separate the two entities. The fence you see on your right enclosed a portion of Lafayette Square across from the White House during the time of the battle. It was moved here in 1933 to separate the two cemeteries.

The Gettysburg National Cemetery has also become something of an arboretum, with a wide variety of trees. Each species of tree is marked and it would be a fun exercise to see if you can identify the species by its leaves and profile.

The first fence between the two cemeteries was built in 1864. It was 1726 feet long and cost $2.25 per linear foot. (lg)

Stop 5 – The 1st United States Artillery, Battery H Memorial

The 1st U. S. Artillery, Battery H was commanded by Lt. Chandler Eakin until he was wounded on July 2 and replaced by Lt. Philip Mason. (lg)

The right gun of this battery calls for closer examination. Look at its muzzle and you will see it was made by the "Revere Copper Co." This is the same Revere who warned citizens of Lexington and other villages outside Boston of the British arrival in 1775. His company went on to craft a number of items, including cannon for the war effort. This piece is also unique because its barrel is mounted upside down on its carriage.

This battery was composed of four Napoleon cannons. The tubes of these cannon were smooth (feel inside the barrel) and were therefore used as giant shotguns when the enemy was getting close. They often fired canister rounds, which when exploded, blew out 27 small balls devastating enemy troop formations.

Stop 6 – Soldiers National Monument

Walk along the path to the Soldiers' National Monument on your left. The monument was completed in 1869, making it the second-oldest memorial on the battlefield (you will see the oldest shortly). Randolph Rogers sculpted the four seated figures at the base of the monument. The one holding a sheath of wheat represents Ceres, the Goddess of Plenty. Cleo holds a book and pen and represents history. The Union soldier symbolizes war and the man holding a hammer represents peace. Pay special attention to the chairs as each is detailed with a wealth of symbolism. The Genius of Liberty stands above all clutching the sword of war and the laurel wreath of victory. A Kentucky state

Landscape designer William Saunders wanted to create a park-like environment in the Soldiers' Cemetery. Scores of trees are marked with a descriptive marker. (lg)

Four figures grace the bottom of the Soldiers' Monument. The "War" figure features a Union soldier who fought to bring peace. (lg)

The "History" figure represents a woman recording the soldiers' achievements using a tablet and stylus. (lg)

The "Plenty" figure shows a woman holding a sheaf of wheat representing peace and abundance as a result of the soldiers' efforts. (lg)

This figure is of a mechanic holding a mallet in his right hand representing "Peace." (lg)

monument lies close by. Although no units from Kentucky fought at Gettysburg, the monument celebrates Lincoln, who was its native son.

Immediately after the cemetery's dedication/consecration, many believed this was the site of the platform where Lincoln gave his immortal speech. More recent scholarship places it in the Evergreen Cemetery, on the other side of the fence, not far from the flag which represents Jenny Wade's grave.

Turn around and face the grave sites. You will see the graves are arranged in a large semicircle with each of the 18 states whose sons died here occupying a specific site. The headstones are low and abut each other. The state markers are raised

Dedicated in 1975, "Kentucky honors her son" bears the Bluegrass State's seal and reproduces the Gettysburg Address. It sits in the national cemetery near the base of the soldiers' monument. (cm)

and indicate the number of bodies buried within its section. There are two rings of graves: the states with the largest number of graves form the outer ring (e.g., Maine, Michigan, New York, Pennsylvania, Massachusetts, Ohio, Indiana, and two sections for the unknown soldiers). The rest of the states are located on the inside (e.g., Illinois, West Virginia, Delaware, Rhode Island, New Hampshire, Vermont, New Jersey, Wisconsin, Connecticut, Minnesota, Maryland, and the U.S. Regulars). Of the 3,512 bodies buried in this part of the cemetery, 979 could not be identified by name or by state and are buried in the three sections for the unknown corpses.

Stop 7 – Outer Ring of Graves

Walk back to the plaque with the beginning of the poem and continue to the right along the outer ring of graves—which are now on your left. The first section contains the graves of the unknowns. They are actually buried in three sections. The graves of the unknown from each state are also buried with their comrades.

You will pass the **Indiana** graves and then **Ohio's.** Among the 131 men buried in the Ohio section is the grave of Private George Nixon of the 73rd Ohio Infantry. Yes, he is related to former president Richard Nixon—his great grandfather. He is buried in the row closest to you in grave #4.

The **Massachusetts** portion of the cemetery has 159 grave sites, but not all of them were killed at Gettysburg. Walk over to the second row and look for Private Jeremiah Danforth's grave (#29), Private Charles Trask's (#30), and

After consideration and discussion, the dead were grouped according to state. Each has the number of dead buried in its section. (lg)

Private Charles Wellington's (#31). These men were all part of Co. K of the 13th Massachusetts Infantry who died of their wounds after the battle of Antietam (September 1862) and were initially buried at Chambersburg, Pennsylvania. With the formation of the Gettysburg National Cemetery, the state of Massachusetts moved the bodies here to lie among their comrades.

Two other burials in this section were mistakes. Private John Johnson of the 11th Mississippi Infantry (third row, #1) and Private N. B. Hindman of the 13th Mississippi Infantry (first row, #8) were mistakenly thought to be from Massachusetts and buried in this section. Both died at Camp Letterman, the large Union hospital and each was buried with a headboard bearing his name and unit. Weathering of the temporary headboard near the hospital or an outright mistake in lettering could have caused these errors.

The **Pennsylvania** section has the second-largest number of graves (534) and is dominated by a large memorial to Major General Charles Collis. Collis was the colonel of the 114th Pennsylvania Infantry that fought at the Peach Orchard on July 2. Collis was ill and not with his men at Gettysburg, but the battle affected him so much that he built

If the Charles Collis Memorial seems out of place among the simple rows of Union graves, it is: it is the only personal monument in the cemetery. It took special permission from the Secretary of War to place the monument here in 1906. (lg)

a large home on Seminary Ridge in 1900. As a veteran, Collis could have been buried at Arlington National Cemetery or elsewhere in this cemetery, but he was able to pull strings and have his body buried among his men who fell at Gettysburg. The nickname of Collis's unit was "Collis Zouaves" because of its colorful uniforms. A number of them were buried here but their identities are unknown. They are designed as "Zouaves" and are buried in the second row of this section (graves #6-12).

Two Confederate soldiers are mistakenly buried in the Pennsylvania section: Private James Aker of the 2nd Mississippi Infantry and Sgt. Thomas Graves of the 21st Georgia Infantry. They are both buried in the fourth row (graves #26 and #30). How they got here is unclear. In some cases, it was because the name of the Confederate corpse's home state was similar to a Northern one, but this was not the case here. It is possible that both men were wearing accouterments, such as belt-buckles from the state of Pennsylvania. Two other Confederates are also buried in this section.

New York has the highest number of graves (861). Two noteworthy men are buried in this section. Lieutenant Colonel Max Thoman, commander of the 59th New York, was mortally wounded during the second day's fighting along Cemetery Ridge and is buried in the last row (grave #70). He has the distinction of being the highest ranking officer killed at Gettysburg to be buried in this cemetery. He was only 31 years of age.

Another noteworthy grave in this section is Sgt. Amos Humiston's of the 154th New York Infantry which fought at Kuhn's brickyard on July 1. His body was found on North Stratton Street without identification save the ambrotype of

three children clutched in his hand. This set off a nationwide search for the corpse's identity. The mystery was solved when his widow, Philandra Humiston, came forward. His grave is in the second row (grave #14). You can easily find it by looking for the more traditional gravestones radiating out from the New York Monument.

The marble urn was installed by the surviving members of the 1st Minnesota regiment during the fall of 1867. It would take another 12 years before another state monument was installed at the cemetery. (lg)

Michigan is represented with 171 graves. This plot shows the difficulty of keeping track of the identity of the corpses. One of the men in the 5th Michigan Infantry, Private William Cole, has three burial sites—row closest to you (grave #11), fifth row grave (#14), and seventh row (grave #4). We don't know which grave site he occupies or the identities of the men buried in the other two. All three probably had something on their bodies identifying them as Cole. Two other soldiers in this plot (Private Artimus Clark and Lt. Gilbert Dickey) have two grave sites each.

Continue walking

Those unidentified soldiers whose remains could be narrowed down to a specific state were buried in their state's section. Those without any identification were buried in three sections. (lg)

along the ring and you will come to the section of **Maine** grave sites. Many of the men buried here are from the 20th Maine, who gallantly defended Little Round Top on the late afternoon of July 2. Walk to the row closest to you and head left to grave #13. This is the gravesite of Sgt. William Jordan—a member of the 2nd Maine Infantry whose members mutinied because of a misunderstanding about the expiration of their military service. All but six members joined the 20th Maine and fought at Gettysburg.

Stop 8 – Inner Ring of Graves

Now head back toward the other side of the Soldiers Monument and walk along the path designating the inner ring of graves. These states are here because they lost fewer men than those we just examined.

The first plot is dedicated to the **United States Regulars**. Find the first row of graves and look for Private Henry Gooden's of the 127th U.S.

Colored Troops (grave #30). Although no African American regiments fought at Gettysburg, many were mustered into service, beginning in 1863. Private Gooden saw limited action in Texas and was buried here after he died in 1876.

As a border state, **Maryland** sent men to both armies and one, Private George Barger of the 1st Maryland Potomac Home Guard, is buried in the middle row (grave #2). Nearby (first row, closest to monument) is the grave site of Private Ninion Knott of the 2nd Maryland Battalion (grave #4), a Confederate unit. Both outfits saw action on Culp's Hill on July 3, although they probably did not fight each other.

Continue walking to the **Minnesota** section with 52 graves. The urn here is the oldest monument on the entire battlefield. It was placed here in

1867 by the survivors of the 1st Minnesota Infantry. Although the only unit hailing from the state, it sustained the highest percentage of casualties during what was essentially a suicide attack on July 2. The attack blunted the Confederate breakthrough in the center of the Union line and is credited with helping save the day for Meade's army. What was left of the regiment was thrown forward to help stem the Pickett-Pettigrew-Trimble Charge on July 3. In all, only 18 percent of the men who marched to Gettysburg survived the battle. Interestingly, the urn contains a quote, not from Lincoln's Gettysburg Address, but from Edward Everett's oration.

Continue walking to the **New Jersey** section where you will find some graves on the second row from the monument with only the initials of the

The State of New York lost more men at Gettysburg than any other. It contains the inscription: "To the officers and soldiers of the State of New York who fell in the Battle of Gettysburg, July 1, 2, 3, 1863, many of whom are here buried, this monument is erected by a grateful commonwealth." (lg)

corpse inscribed on the headstone. We now know who they are: James Flavigar (grave #6), Martin Van Housten (grave #19), and Henry Rourke (grave #21).

Corporal John Ackerman of the 82nd Illinois Infantry is buried in grave #5 of the **Illinois** section. Like many men, Ackerman had a strong premonition this battle would be his last. He begged off joining his unit as they advanced into the fields north of Gettysburg on July 1, but was later found with half a head—killed by an exploding Confederate artillery shell.

Stop 9 – New York State Monument

Continue to the path and turn left and head to the New York State Monument. This 94-foot-high monument crafted in granite was dedicated in 1893. The figure at the top holds a wreath to place over a grave. One cannot easily see that the figure is weeping for the 6,700 Empire State soldiers who became casualties during the three-day battle. Further down the shaft, one can see an eagle in front of banners and weapons and continuing down is a bas relief of the fighting representing four seminal aspects of the battle—death of John Reynolds, wounding of Winfield Hancock, wounding of Dan Sickles and Henry Slocum's Council

Until the cemetery closed for additional burials, 3,307 men chose to be buried at the cemetery. Their headstones are more "traditional" and easier to identify. (lg)

of War. Four tablets line the base of the monument that identify the New York officers killed at Gettysburg and provide symbols of the seven army corps that fought here. After the Pennsylvania Memorial, it is the second largest on the battlefield.

Stop 10 – John Reynolds Statue

First Corps commander, John Fulton Reynolds, actually has three monuments on the Gettysburg battlefield. The others are along Chambersburg Pike on McPherson's Ridge and just south of it, marking the approximate location of his mortal wounding. This statue was crafted from four bronze cannon barrels. (lg)

Two statues of General John Reynolds grace the battlefield. Most visitors see the large sculpture of Reynolds atop a horse along Chambersburg Pike, where his I Corps desperately fought during July 1 to keep the growing Confederate presence at bay until additional Union troops arrived. Reynolds gave his life early in the battle. A second statue to Reynolds is here, in the National Cemetery. Ironically, John Reynolds never visited Cemetery Hill, but the survivors of the I Corps saw fit to place a monument of him in the National Cemetery. This was the first bronze statue on the Gettysburg battlefield, being dedicated in 1872. It was crafted by sculptor John Quincy Adams Ward using four bronze cannon barrels melted down to create this statue.

Stop 12 – Edgell's Battery

You might wish to take a short side-trip to the right to see the Masonic Friend to Friend Memorial. Take the path just after the 75th Ohio monument and you will come to the Masonic Memorial. It shows Confederate general Lewis Armistead being assisted by fellow-Mason, Capt. Hiram Bingham. This memorial was produced using a polychrome patina process causing various color variations that change depending upon light conditions. There are also a number of symbolic objects on the memorial, including a fly, which

The "Friend To Friend" Masonic Memorial was crafted by Ron Tunison and dedicated in 1993. Tunison crafted several other Gettysburg monuments, such as the Delaware State Monument, the statue of Gen. Samuel Crawford, and the Women's Memorial. (lg)

symbolizes death and destruction, a butterfly for life after death, a cannonball to connote the actions of the battle, particularly since Armistead was mortally wounded near Cushing's battery, and a Union and Confederate bullet.

Walk back the way you came and continue along the path toward the entrance of the cemetery. You will pass many graves of the Civil War veterans and those who fought in other battlefields.

Stop 11 – The Masonic Memorial (Optional)

This attractive monument is topped with a granite representation of the type of shell fired by these cannon.

You have now completed the cemetery tour.

Please be careful crossing the road to the parking area.

The 1st New Hampshire Light Artillery Battery was commanded by Capt. Frederick M. Edgell during the battle. It assumed this position at 4:00 p.m. on July 2 and later moved south to help stop the evening attack on Cemetery Hill. The battery returned to this position and was instrumental in repulsing the Pickett-Pettigrew-Trimble Charge on July 3. (lg)

The Gettysburg Address Turns 100

APPENDIX C

BY CHRIS MACKOWSKI

For the 100th anniversary of the Gettysburg Address, the U. S. Civil War Centennial Commission and National Park Service invited President John F. Kennedy to come to south-central Pennsylvania and offer a few appropriate remarks. Kennedy was renowned for his writing almost as much as Lincoln was—he had won the Pulitzer Prize for Biography in 1957 for *Profiles in Courage*, and his inaugural address had become an instant classic—so the president seemed the ideal choice for such an auspicious occasion. He had also visited the battlefield earlier that year, in March, and had enjoyed himself tremendously.

Kennedy demurred on a return trip, however. He had already committed to attend a political event in Dallas, Texas, at the request of Vice President Lyndon B. Johnson. Kennedy sent, in his stead, (very) brief remarks:

> *On this solemn occasion let us all rededicate ourselves to the perpetuation of those ideals of which Lincoln spoke so luminously. As Americans, we can do no less.*

Imagine how history might have unfolded differently had JFK gone to Gettysburg in November 1963 instead of Dallas.

With JFK unavailable, the Civil War Centennial Commission cast about for an appropriate substitute. As it happened, the next-most prominent figure from American politics happened to already live in Gettysburg: JFK's predecessor in the White House, General Dwight D. Eisenhower. Eisenhower and his wife, Mamie, had purchased a farm on the outskirts of the battlefield in 1950 and, following Ike's presidency, they had moved to the farm permanently for a quiet retirement.

"Gettysburg always loomed large for Ike," explains historian Dan Vermilya, who works at the farm, now preserved as the Eisenhower National Historic site. "Eisenhower had long said after his military career he wanted to retire as a farmer, and their Gettysburg farm was an idyllic setting for such a goal. Of course, it helped that the farm they bought shared a boundary with the

Eisenhower National Historic Site preserves 690.5 acres and a 4,100-square foot home with 24 rooms. It retains 99 percent of the Eisenhowers's original furnishings. (lg)

Although JFK could not attend the centennial ceremony because of a prior commitment in Dallas, Texas, he had visited the battlefield on March 31, 1863. Seeing the Peace Light Memorial on Oak Hill inspired Kennedy's wife, Jackie, to install an "eternal flame" on JFK's grave following the president's assassination. (gg)

Gettysburg battlefield. The former general never could escape war, or studying it, even in his retirement."

Ike even surrendered the honorific title "Mr. President" in favor of "General" when Congress restored his military rank upon his retirement from politics.

When the Centennial Commission extended the invitation to Ike to deliver the keynote at the commemoration ceremony, Eisenhower gladly accepted. He'd spoken there already on June 30, 1963, in recognition of the centennial of the battle, but the chance to commemorate the dedication of the cemetery presented an especially meaningful opportunity. "When he commanded troops at Camp Colt in Gettysburg in 1918, Ike frequently went to the National Cemetery to read the Gettysburg Address to himself near the spot where Lincoln delivered it," Vermilya says.

Dwight D. Eisenhower, former leader of the free world, now gentleman farmer. (nps)

Events that November 19 began with a VIP luncheon at the Gettysburg Hotel, where Dr. James I. Robertson, executive director of the Centennial Commission, offered a few remarks. From there, the *Gettysburg Times* reported, dignitaries climbed into a dozen "sleek sedans," with Ike and Pennsylvania Governor Bill Scranton in the lead car. Mamie Eisenhower was there, too, "dressed in brilliant red and displaying her famous smile."

The procession left Lincoln Square and went down Baltimore Street, then turned onto Steinwehr Avenue., and eventually onto the Taneytown Road. "One hundred years ago they rode in carriages or on horseback," the newspaper noted. "There was not a horse in Tuesday's parade." There was, however, the U.S. Marine Band, "resplendent in their scarlet and silver braid dress uniforms," marching at the head of the column just as their counterparts had done a century earlier.

"The weather Tuesday was as pleasant as it was in 1863," the newspaper noted, with the temperature reaching 59 degrees. As the crowd gathered in the cemetery, everyone enjoying the "bright sunlight that fell generously and warmly." The newspaper estimated some 10,000 spectators attended the ceremony.

Despite the similarity in the weather, the landscape had changed—aged—in the century since the cemetery was established. "One hundred years ago there was no stone fence and no tall trees towering beyond it," the correspondent wrote. "The cemetery was a converted cornfield and all of the trees have grown to their stature since the dedication day."

All went smoothly during the ceremony. Singer Marian Anderson performed, and E. Washington Rhodes, editor-publisher of the *Philadelphia Tribune* and president of the National Newspaper Publishers Association, offered remarks. Rhodes acknowledged 1963 as a "time of racial tension and unrest" and in that context recognized his appearance at the lectern as "a historic moment of high honor and drama," reported the *New York Times.*

Rhodes "called emphatically for statesmanship like Lincoln's to replace the racial antipathies, political expediency, sectional hatreds and 'walls of hostile silence....' He would declare that men of substance and creative minds must take action, move forward with alertness and stout hearts to remove this injustice, lest government of the people, by the people and for the people be endangered beyond repair."

Governor Scranton, at his turn at the microphone, struck an optimistic tone. "[T]he tyranny of prejudice is doomed because the American people in their deep common sense realize it is wrong," he said. According to the *Times*, Scranton noted that the day's gathering had not been convoked for the sake of Lincoln "but for our own sake, as free men, to refresh ourselves at this shrine—to find increased devotion for the unfinished cause of human freedom."

Finally, "The General" rose to speak.

The Eisenhowers donated their property to the National Park Service in 1967; although Ike died in 1969, Maime lived on the property until her own death in 1979. The NPS opened the site in 1980. (nps)

"We mark today the centennial of an immortal address," Ike said:

We stand where Abraham Lincoln stood as, a century ago, he gave to the world words as moving in their solemn cadence as they are timeless in their meaning. Little wonder it is that, as here we sense his deep dedication to freedom, our own dedication takes added strength.

Lincoln had faith that the ancient drums of Gettysburg, throbbing mutual defiance from the battle lines of the blue and the gray, would one day beat in unison, to summon a people, happily united in peace, to fulfill, generation by generation, a noble destiny. His faith has been justified—but the unfinished work of which he spoke in 1863 is still unfinished; because of human frailty, it always will be.

Where we see the serenity with which time has invested this hallowed ground, Lincoln saw the scarred earth and felt the press of personal grief. Yet he lifted his eyes to the future, the future that is our present. He foresaw a new birth of freedom, a freedom and equality for all which, under God, would restore the purpose and meaning of America, defining a goal that challenges each of us to attain his full stature of citizenship.

We read Lincoln's sentiments, we ponder his words—the beauty of the sentiments he expressed enthralls us; the majesty of his words holds us spellbound – but we have not paid to his message its just tribute until we—ourselves—live it. For well he knew that to live for country is a duty, as demanding as is the readiness to die for it. So long as this truth remains our guiding light, self-government in this nation will never die.

True to democracy's basic principle that all are created equal and endowed by the Creator with priceless human rights, the good citizen now, as always before, is called upon to defend the rights of others as he does his own; to subordinate self to the country's good; to refuse to take the easy way today that may invite national disaster tomorrow; to accept the truth that the work still to be done awaits his doing.

On this day of commemoration, Lincoln still asks of each of us, as clearly as he did of those who heard his words a century ago, to give that increased devotion to the cause for which soldiers in all our wars have given the last full measure of devotion. Our answer, the only worthy one we can render to the memory of the great emancipator, is ever to defend, protect and pass on unblemished, to coming generations the heritage—the trust—that Abraham Lincoln,

Thousands showed up on a beautiful November day to hear Ike's speech. (nps)

Eisenhower, at the lectern, is flanked by dignitaries. Singer Marian Anderson, the only woman on stage, is near the left edge of the photo. Speaker E. Washington Rhodes is on the far right of the photo. Standing next to him is Pennsylvania Governor Bill Scranton. (nps)

and all the ghostly legions of patriots of the past, with unflinching faith in their God, have bequeathed to us—a nation free, with liberty, dignity, and justice for all.

Ike's speech "contained many themes that Ike spoke on throughout his life," Vermilya points out. "Eisenhower believed very deeply in the importance of active citizenship, that it was up to each one of us to do our part in preserving democracy. That was a central feature in Lincoln's Gettysburg Address, and it shines through in Ike's speech commemorating the moment 100 years later."

When Ike finished speaking, the crowd rose to its feet in standing ovation. "[T]here were many moments when those in the audience swallowed hard several times as lumps arose in their throats . . ." the newspaper reported, "and there were obvious glistening of tears. . . ."

Ike is not necessarily remembered for his eloquence as a speaker, but as the man who led the Allies to victory in World War II, Ike knew the truth of Lincoln's words. He, if anyone, understood the full weight of sacrifice made by those who have given "the last full measure of devotion."

Lincoln's Gettysburg Address has become arguably the most famous speech in American history, and during the centennial celebration, "every word of the speech was analyzed and explained by historians, politicians, journalists and foreign diplomats," the *New York Times* reported. It's little wonder, then, that Ike's words commemorating that speech have been entirely overshadowed by the original, immortal text. However, Ike's words, like Lincoln's, still resonate today. We are the "coming generations" Ike referred to.

The work still to be done awaits our doing.

CHRIS MACKOWSKI *is the editor-in-chief of Emerging Civil War. He teaches writing in St. Bonaventure University's Jandoli School of Communication. He is also historian-in-residence at Stevenson Ridge, a historic property.*

Suggested Reading

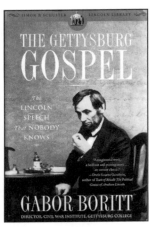

The Gettysburg Gospel: The Lincoln Speech that Nobody Knows
Gabor Boritt
Simon & Schuster, 2006
ISBN: 978-0743288200

A classic rendition of the Soldiers' Cemetery, Lincoln's speech, and the events taking place during this period.

The Gettysburg Soldiers' Cemetery and Lincoln's Address: Aspects and Angles
Frank L. Klement
White Mane Publishing Company, 1993
ISBN: 978-0942597615

A wonderful collection of articles on many facets of the Soldiers' Cemetery, the Consecration Ceremony, and Lincoln's role in it.

Writing the Gettysburg Address
Martin P. Johnson
University of Kansas Press, 2013
ISBN: 978-0-7006-1933-7

A highly readable scholarly account of how Lincoln crafted the Gettysburg Address and the meaning behind it.

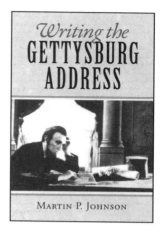

Lincoln at Gettysburg: The Words that Remade America
Garry Wills
Simon & Schuster, 2006
ISBN: 978-0743299633

A scholarly approach to Lincoln's Gettysburg Address

Revised Report made to the Legislature of Pennsylvania Relative to the Soldiers' National Cemetery at Gettysburg
Singerly & Myers, 1867
Available via archive.org

Contains a wealth of information about the Cemetery and its Consecration

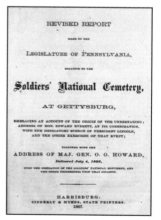

About the Authors

Bradley M. Gottfried served as a college educator for more than 40 years before he retired in 2017. After receiving his doctorate, he taught for eleven years and then entered the administrator ranks, rising to the position of president, serving for 17 years at two colleges. His interest in the Civil War began when he was a youngster in the Philadelphia area. He has written 14 books on the Civil War, including a number on Gettysburg as well as several map studies of various campaigns. A resident of the Chambersburg, Pennsylvania area, Brad is an Antietam Licensed Battlefield Guide and a Gettysburg Licensed Town Guide.

Linda I. Gottfried served as a graphic designer and development officer at several colleges and nonprofit organizations before retiring in 2015. She is now a full-time sculptor. Several of her pieces have won awards.

The Gottfrieds contribute their time to assisting nonprofit organizations in crafting strategic plans and assistance in planning effective fundraising initiatives.

The Gottfrieds have four children and six grandchildren.